The Wit & Wisdom *of* Jane Goodall

The Wit & Wisdom *of* Jane Goodall

CHAS NEWKEY-BURDEN

Gaia

First published in Great Britain in 2026 by Gaia, an imprint of
Octopus Publishing Group Ltd
Carmelite House
50 Victoria Embankment
London EC4Y 0DZ
www.octopusbooks.co.uk

An Hachette UK Company
www.hachette.co.uk

The authorized representative in the EEA is Hachette Ireland,
8 Castlecourt Centre, Dublin 15, D15 XTP3, Ireland (email: info@hbgi.ie)

Illustrations by Montse Bernal

ISBN 978-1-85675-609-9
eISBN 978-1-85675-610-5

A CIP catalogue record for this book is available from the British Library.

Typeset in 11.5/17pt Plantin MT Pro by
Six Red Marbles UK, Thetford, Norfolk

Printed and bound in Great Britain.

1 3 5 7 9 10 8 6 4 2

This FSC® label means that materials used for the
product have been responsibly sourced.

FSC www.fsc.org MIX Paper | Supporting responsible forestry FSC® C104740

Dedicated to the divine Lalita of New Gokul Farm

Contents

Introduction

Few people have changed the way we see the natural world as profoundly as Jane Goodall. Through her groundbreaking research with chimpanzees, her tireless commitment to conservation, and her humane and spiritual outlook on life, she has inspired generations to reconsider humanity's relationship with animals, nature and each other.

When Jane first arrived in Africa in the 1960s to begin her study of wild chimpanzees, she was not yet a trained scientist. Instead, she brought with her a rare combination of patience, curiosity and compassion – qualities that would soon revolutionize the study of animal behaviour.

Working under the mentorship of the renowned anthropologist Louis Leakey, she set out to observe chimpanzees in their natural environment. What she discovered would change our understanding of the boundary between humans and other animals.

She observed chimpanzees making and using tools, an ability previously thought to be uniquely human. But her observations did more than expand scientific knowledge; they invited the world to look at animals not as distant, inferior creatures but as fellow beings sharing our planet. No wonder she became a global icon.

But Jane herself was never one to seek recognition, which perhaps makes it all the more important that we celebrate her. We will do so by remembering the wit and wisdom of this remarkable woman – someone who made us think, made us laugh, and ultimately helped us change the way we see the world. As we will discover, she was every bit as witty as she was wise. Along the way, we will explore some of the fascinating stories and little-known moments from her extraordinary life.

At a time when the challenges facing our planet can feel overwhelming, Jane's voice offers something essential: perspective. Her life demonstrates that meaningful change often begins with curiosity, courage and compassion. Through her words, we are reminded that every individual has the capacity to make a difference, and that the future of our planet is shaped not only by global powers but by the simple choices we make each day.

I have been a lifelong lover of animals, and in my role as a writer and campaigner for animal rights, Jane's empathy and passion for the natural world have always resonated deeply with me. My hope is that this book will be more than simply a celebration of her life. By sharing her story, I hope it also becomes an invitation – to think more deeply, to care more widely, and to act more thoughtfully in our relationship with Mother Nature and all her treasures.

A Timeline of Jane Goodall's Life

1934 Born Valerie Jane Morris-Goodall at 11:30pm on 3 April 1934, in a nursing home in Hampstead Heath, North London. Four years to the day later, her sister Judy was born.

1939–1945 Spent time with her grandmother in the English countryside during World War II, where her love for wildlife was deepened, even as battles raged.

1952 Left school, moved to London and took various jobs to save money to travel to Africa.

1957 Made her first trip to Africa and began work at Olduvai Gorge. She met the famous paleoanthropologist Louis Leakey, who spotted her observational skills and hired her as a secretary and assistant.

1960 Began her studies at Gombe Stream Game Reserve. She spotted chimpanzee David Greybeard fishing for termites and saw chimps eating meat. She also noticed chimpanzees using tools, overturning the belief that only humans make tools.

1962 Went to Cambridge University in the UK to begin work on her PhD.

1963 *National Geographic* published its first cover story about Jane and her research.

1964 Married the wildlife photographer Hugo van Lawick, whom she'd met the previous year. Their son, Hugo Eric Louis (nicknamed 'Grub'), would be born in 1967, and the couple would divorce in 1974.

1965 Received her PhD in Ethology from Cambridge University – only the eighth person to receive the degree without having a bachelor's degree.

1975 Married her second husband, Derek Bryceson, a former member of Tanzania's parliament and the director of its national parks.

1977 Founded the Jane Goodall Institute to support research, conservation and education.

1980 Began to speak more widely about conservation and the destruction of chimpanzee habitat. Bryceson died of cancer.

1995 Received the title of Dame Commander of the Order of the British Empire (DBE) from Elizabeth II.

1999 Her book *Reason for Hope: A Spiritual Journey* was published.

2004 Officially invested as Dame Jane Goodall by Elizabeth II at Buckingham Palace. In the same year, she was also named a UN Messenger of Peace by Secretary-General Kofi Annan.

2006 The programme *Jane Goodall's Heroes* was launched on Animal Planet.

2010 A documentary film about her life, *Jane's Journey,* premiered.

2014 A species of orchid discovered in New Guinea was named after her: *Dendrobium goodallianum*.

2015 Endorsed the Green Party candidate, Caroline Lucas, in the run up to the UK general election.

2018 World Chimpanzee Day was established to raise awareness for the care, protection and conservation of chimpanzees in the wild and in captivity.

2021 *The Book of Hope* was published, in which Jane shared her reasons for optimism.

2022 A doll of Goodall, made from recycled plastic, was launched as part of the Barbie Inspiring Women series.

2024 The world celebrated Jane's ninetieth birthday with events and activities throughout the year. Despite her advanced years, Jane continued to travel around 300 days each year.

2025 Died in her sleep of natural causes on 1 October 2025 during a speaking tour of the United States. Jane was staying at the home of a friend in Beverly Hills, California. She was ninety-one. Her funeral was held on 12 November and over one thousand five hundred people gathered at Washington National Cathedral in Washington, DC.

Chapter One

Early Years

1934–1959

'But what is the beginning? Is it the moment when I was born, with all the charming ugliness of the newborn human baby, in a hospital in London?'

—Jane Goodall in *Reason for Hope: A Spiritual Journey*[1]

The Beginnings of Jane Goodall

The remarkable life of Jane Goodall began on 3 April 1934, when she was born in Hampstead, North London. It was quite a year for famous births: Jane appeared in the world in the same year as the actors Judi Dench, Brigitte Bardot and Richard Briers, the cosmonaut Yuri Gagarin and the musician Leonard Cohen.

Her birth name was Valerie Jane Morris-Goodall. Her father was Mortimer Herbert Morris-Goodall, a businessman who followed in his family's footsteps. Mortimer's grandfather, Charles Goodall (born on 4 December 1785 in Northampton) was a manufacturer of playing cards. Later, his descendants expanded the operation to include almanacs, calendars and menu cards. The company trademark was the family name, split to form the words 'good' and 'all' in the shape of a heart.

Her mother was Margaret Myfanwe Joseph, an author from Milford Haven, Pembrokeshire.

Margaret was the daughter of a Congregational minister in Bournemouth. She had trained as a secretary and worked in London, also writing novels under the pen name of Vanne Morris-Goodall (the name she was called by her family). Margaret once remarked that she became a writer because she loved the process of writing and finding the correct words to describe events. The attempts of young men to charm Margaret with their words were less successful. One day she was told that her hair was 'like burnished chestnut'. Another charmer told her she was a 'green-eyed goddess'.

When Margaret gave birth to her daughter Jane, the Prime Minister of the United Kingdom was James Ramsay MacDonald, King George V was on the throne, and the average weekly wage was between £2 and £3.

The UK was experiencing mixed fortunes at the time: it was the depths of the Great Depression, with high unemployment in industrial areas, low wages and economic hardship. But there were some signs of new social improvements such as new housing and growing car ownership. In the 1930s, one-third of women in the UK worked outside the home – mostly in low-paid 'women's jobs', such as caring and cooking.

During the year of Jane's birth, the penguin pool was opened at London Zoo, the first Dinky toys were launched, and the wedding of Prince George, Duke of Kent, to Princess Marina of Greece and Denmark became the first royal nuptials to be broadcast live on radio. Further afield, Adolf Hitler became Germany's dictator, or Führer. The global population was around 2.1 billion.

★ ★ ★

Jane was an Aries, the star sign known for being bold, ambitious and independent leaders who dive headfirst into challenges. Their purported weaknesses are believed to be impatience, moodiness, impulsiveness and aggression. The positive attributes of the star sign are the ones

most people would associate with Jane, including honesty, optimism, passion and energy.

Her earliest years were spent in an urban environment but she enjoyed what creatures there were to see in the limited green spaces around her. 'I was born right in the heart of London, where animals were limited to dog and cats, sparrows, pigeons and some insect life in the small garden shared by the inhabitants of the mews where we lived.'[2] A surprising beginning for someone who would go on to work in much more exotic settings.

When Jane was just three weeks old, the family hired a nanny, Nancy Sowden, to look after her. In return for six and a half days of childcare, Sowden was given board and £1 in spending money each week. Looking back, she remembered Jane as a good girl who never needed 'scolding because she never did anything wrong'.[3]

Jane's father was something of a distant figure, a common state of affairs in English families in those comparatively stiff and cold days. He once said that he hadn't see her for about a year because she would already be in bed by the time he got home from work. As for fatherly affection, there was precious little of that.

Despite this lack of interest, as her biographer Dale Peterson wrote, Jane was a bright young woman: 'she grew up to be a woman with a race driver's constitution: good eyesight, high energy, a natural and happy competitiveness, a capacity for intense and extended concentration, a surprising attraction to risk, and an unusual tolerance for physical stress and oscillatory motion.'[4]

In her childhood home at 2 Clabon Mews in London, she enjoyed playing with her younger sister, Judy. Elder siblings like Jane are supposed to be more extroverted, agreeable and conscientious, their younger siblings more fun-loving, outgoing and creative, but the two Goodall sisters were certainly close and spent a lot of time together. The highlights for Jane usually involved nature.

'When we were small, my sister Judy and I had a story read to us every night. There was one I loved about the time when the birds decided to have a competition to see who would fly the highest.'[5]

But the girls could be naughty. 'We had lots of fun disobeying the rules,'[6] Jane told Dale Peterson. But this didn't mean she necessarily misunderstood the reason for the rules, which she felt were fair and reasonable.

Jane was born with prosopagnosia, a neurological condition which makes it difficult to recognize familiar faces. Only later did she discover that this was a condition that her own sister, Judy, also experienced. Jane said it was embarrassing and curiously humbling to suffer from the condition as it made social occasions awkward. Her understanding of it evolved over the years.

'I used to think it was due to some mental laziness, and I tried desperately to memorize the faces of people I met so that, if I saw them the next day, I would recognize them,' she wrote. She had 'no trouble with those who had obvious physical characteristics – unusual bone structure, beaky nose, extreme beauty or the opposite',[7] but with other faces she failed miserably. Never would she have thought as a child that she was destined for the spotlight.

> Did You Know?
>
> When Jane's shoes began to wear out, she put brown paper inside them because the family couldn't afford to get them cobbled. She would giggle about this, she remembered.

An Early Love for Animals

From the time she could crawl, Jane was fascinated by animals. At just a year old, she was given a toy chimpanzee, named Jubilee, instead of a teddy bear. It proved quite a controversial gift. She recalls a time when her mother's friend saw the monkey and was horrified at such a toy, thinking it would have given a small girl of her age horrible nightmares. In fact, Jubilee became her favourite toy and sparked her lifelong love of animals. She loved Jubilee so much that she kept it her whole life.

In time, Jubilee would become a shining star in its own right as part of a touring exhibition, organized by the National Geographic Society and the Jane Goodall Institute. The exhibition also included an audio recording of her mother's voice. Revisiting Vanne's voice two decades after her death really moved Goodall. 'It really gave shivers up my back hearing her voice like that. I wasn't expecting that,' she said.[8]

Jane also began to play with the living creatures that fascinated her. Sometimes, this led to a swift lesson in animal welfare for the girl who would go on to teach the world how to treat animals well. At the age of eighteen months, Jane collected a handful of earthworms from their garden and took them to bed with her. She didn't want to be apart from them, but when her mother Vanne explained that the worms would die if she kept them there, Jane returned them to the garden.

★ ★ ★

Jane was born with a love for all nature, and she was particularly in tune with her environment on a sensory level. Once when she was asked what her first 'scent memory' was, she recalled the earthy smell of freshly turned soil as it was tied to her childhood fascination of earthworms, which she was always digging up. Another scent that she loved was of freshly mowed grass as it evoked a strong sense of nostalgia for her. She also loved the smell of lily of the valley, which reminded her of the flowers that grew in her garden as a child. Similarly, the smell of spring violets in bloom brought back the same vivid emotions and connections to her childhood and early experiences.

One of her earliest memories was the time she hid in a small stuffy henhouse to discover how a

hen laid an egg. 'I had always wondered where on a hen was an opening big enough for the egg to come out,' she explained. Finally, after hours of waiting, she got her answer. When she eventually emerged a little dishevelled some five hours later, she found out that her mother had rung the police to report her as missing. 'So now I know how a hen lays an egg', she told her mother excitedly. Despite Jane's unorthodox curiosity, her mother was always supportive.[9]

And like so much of what happened during her life, Goodall drew a positive lesson from it. Recalling the story of the hens, Jane said, 'If you look at that story with hindsight, isn't that the making of a little scientist? The curiosity, asking questions, not getting the answer you want, deciding to find out for yourself, making a mistake, not giving up, and having patience. It was all there!'[10] Jane continued to recount the hen story for the rest of her life, often choosing the highly evocative word 'plop' to describe exactly how the egg emerged.

Jane also fell in love with cows, among other animals, from an early age. 'I first met cows when I was five years old, on a farm belonging to my father's family,' she said. 'I remember I was so excited to see the cows and their calves out in a big field, the mothers grazing while their calves played and frolicked.' Ten years later she would learn to milk cows as a teenager. 'This was in the days when the cows were milked in the morning, let out of the barn to graze all day, then came in from the fields to be milked in the late afternoon,' she said. As we'll see, she continued to love cows and grew horrified by their treatment on modern dairy farms.[11]

★ ★ ★

During her long life, Jane would meet with some of the most accomplished people in their fields and send them away with their minds radically changed by the encounter. This was a skill she seemed to be born with, because even as a small child, she could make a big impact on others. A porter at

Peter Jones department store was unsettled by the toddler Jane. 'She looks straight through me, just as though she knows all my secrets,' he told her nanny.[12]

She also showed from an early age an understanding of how to get her way. At the age of ten, she drafted a mock legal document which was designed to ensure she would inherit her favourite beech tree. It might not have stood up in court but it didn't have to.

But some of the qualities she developed later on came as a bit of a shock to Jane. As a schoolgirl, she had no idea she would end up as a public speaker at all, let alone such a prolific one. 'Because I'm so shy, desperately shy! As a child, I could not stand up in front of my class,' she said. Although she became a very successful speaker, those nerves would never fully desert her.[13]

The household Jane grew up in was not a wealthy one, but a lack of money didn't mean a lack of love. It didn't bother her that they didn't go on expensive holidays or have a car or bicycle; as Jane explained, 'we had enough to eat, some clothes to wear, and an abundance of love, laughter and fun.'[14] And anyway, she was glad to grow up before the age of mass media and digitization because it made her appreciate nature. Would she have lived the life she went on to live had computers and iPhones been around when she was born? Like most children before the age of television and computer games, Jane loved being outdoors where she would play in secret corners of the garden and learn about nature. 'My love of living things was encouraged, so that from the very beginning I was able to develop that sense of wonder, of awe, that can lead to spiritual awareness.'[15] And it was her spirituality that became a significant aspect of her life.

Did You Know?

Of the twenty or so books that Jane wrote for adults and children during her life, four contain the word 'hope' in their title.

Spiritual Beginnings

In their childhood home, Jane and her sister were expected to stay humble and say their prayers at night, kneeling on the floor at the side of the bed. Theirs was a fairly religious household, paving the way for the spiritual and religious consciousness that Jane developed during her life.

One of her favourite sayings was, 'As thy days, so shall thy strength be'. It's from the book of Deuteronomy in the Bible and is generally interpreted as a divine promise that strength and grace are supplied in direct proportion to one's daily needs and trials. It was a source of comfort throughout her life.

Some have interpreted the early passages in Genesis in the Bible as a justification for humanity's power over the animal kingdom, but Jane wasn't so sure. 'Well, the Bible says that man was given dominion over the birds and the beasts and everything, but it's a mistranslation of the Hebrew word,' she said. 'It's not dominion. It's stewardship. That makes a very big difference.' [16]

'We went to church and worshiped God the Father, God the Son, and God the Holy Ghost,' she said in 2003. 'But my wise mother told me that if I'd been born to a Jewish family, I'd worship Jehovah, to a Muslim family, Allah, to a Native American family, the Creator, and so on.'[17] Jane's grandmother was a religious woman whose faith influenced her granddaughter. Rather than calling her 'granny', they called her 'Danny', which seemed a bit easier to pronounce for young children. When Danny died at the age of ninety-seven, it seemed like she had seen her own death in advance, telling her daughter,

'I think you should write my obituary tonight, darling'. The next morning, she was lying peacefully dead. She had tied up all her letters from her late husband and stuck a handwritten note on them that read, 'Please send these with me on my last journey.'[18]

One memory Jane always treasured about Danny was how conciliatory she was. She remembers how Danny had a horror of ending the day without making peace with others around her. Like any household with many people living together, there were always little arguments or domestic rows, but Danny insisted that these squabbles had to be resolved before going to bed. 'Let not the sun set on thy wrath,' Danny would often say – a line from the Bible that stayed in Jane's mind whenever she fought with someone. Danny would often tell Jane how terrible she would feel if she should die before she had said sorry. Perhaps this reality of life's fleetingness was why Jane had such an urgent sense of life's value. She wrote in the words of the poet Walter de la Mare to make the most of every moment in life: 'Look thy last on all things lovely, Every hour.'[19]

However, Jane's positive outlook on the lovely things in life was challenged early in her childhood, and arguably forged her passion to protect the natural world. One day, when she was small, a dragonfly started hovering around her. Suddenly, and seemingly out of nowhere, a man close by intercepted the dragonfly and crushed it to death. This instantly made Jane cry. But she clarified that the tears were not because she was afraid, it was because she felt bad that such a pretty thing was destroyed.[20] Little did she know this act of violence was a sign that life was about to change in a dramatic way.

Did You Know?

When Jane went to stay with her paternal grandmother Danny Nutt in 1942, she wrote her first letter home. Scrawled in pencil, it included tales of a big dog called Jacky, and two porcelain dogs she had been given, named Trouble and Terry. Full of spelling errors, the letter also included tales of a 'ded rook' she had found and her tea, which included a 'bold egg'. Jane concluded, 'I hop you can read this letter'.

A Change in the Air

As we have seen, Jane's father was always a distant figure but when World War II started, Jane saw even less of him. 'I don't remember my father much,' she said. 'War broke out when I was young, then he was gone for good.'[21]

Decades later, she remembered how the family were in London sitting in the living room as they listened to the BBC announce at the start of the nine o'clock news on the radio that Britain had declared war on Nazi Germany. It was a grave and terrifying moment, even for a youngster who couldn't quite understand the consequences of what she was hearing. It left a deep impression on her.

'I was only five, too young to appreciate all that it meant – but it was the tension of the grown-ups, the sense of dread, that forever shaped my views on life and war,' she wrote in 2021. 'After all, we had only recently begun to recover from World War I. Even now, when I hear the chimes of Big Ben – that always preceded the news – I feel an involuntary twinge of – well, almost fear. All these years later.'[22]

When she was five, her father had wanted her and her sister to learn French, so he had moved the family to Le Touquet. But three months later when war broke out, the family returned to England. This meant they never fulfilled their father's wish that they learn French when they were young.

So, back to England it was. But London was out of the question. First, they stayed in Jane's great grandmother's home in the Kent countryside. The house was lit by oil lamps and there were sheep and cows grazing nearby. Then they moved to Bournemouth on the south coast of England, to a home that she would have connections with right into the 2020s. It was a 'rather ramshackle red-brick Victorian house with old-fashioned sash windows and cream-coloured walls', she recalled.[23]

> Did You Know?
>
> Jane's family home in Bournemouth was called The Birches and they kept several cats, guinea pigs, hamsters and turtles there, plus a canary called Peter.

'There was a time when Britain stood alone in Europe against the might of Nazi Germany,'

Jane once told *The Washington Post*. 'The rest of Europe was overrun and defeated, or they capitulated. Actually, there was no good reason for hope. We didn't have the defenses. We hadn't built up an adequate army, navy or air force. But we did have some very brave young men, and we had [Winston] Churchill saying "We'll fight on the beaches, we'll fight in the cities, we'll fight in the lanes and we will not be defeated."'[24]

Like most people who lived through it, World War II shook Jane to the core. Only later did she fully realize how the horror of the war, the Holocaust, and the dropping of atomic bombs had deeply affected her.[25]

She remembers how the blackout dominated their lives every evening and American soldiers with their tanks occupied the road outside The Birches. One of the American soldiers became a real friend, but then went off to the front with his regiment and was, like so many thousands, killed.

The war was tough for Judy but Jane did her best to support her little sister. When Judy was four, she sometimes woke up in tears, exclaiming that Hitler was going to burn down their home. Jane drew her a picture of Hitler burning inside his own home. Judy put this under her pillow and it calmed her down for a few nights. When she started having more nightmares, Jane would draw pictures and write poems for her.

But as much as Jane tried to protect her sister, and in fact they were among the lucky ones that fled London, the signs of war were all around them. It was impossible to ignore. Her own father was far away and in uniform, somewhere in the jungles of Singapore and she remembers Uncle Eric and Aunt Olly setting off on air-raid duty out into the dark night when the air-raid warning sounded. Jane even remembered her own encounter when she saw two bombs dropping from a German plane while they were playing on the coastline. She described how they looked like small cigars in the sky as they dropped to land. It was a close encounter as the bomb made a deep crater halfway up the road, but Jane and her family were safely out of harm's way.

Despite the global suffering and widespread evil of the war years, Jane looked on the bright side and said she was glad she grew up in the war years because she learned to take nothing for granted. 'One square of chocolate was a huge treat. Food was rationed. Clothes were rationed. We had very little money,' she said.[26]

The consciousness of people who grew up during the war is usually quite different to people growing up today, she noticed. But she never blamed the latter group. They were just as shaped by their circumstances as she was by hers. Jane acknowledged that when young people take things for granted in today's world, it's because they don't know anything different.

★ ★ ★

After the war ended, Jane kept a curious memento, one that many people would blanch from owning, but that Jane drew great inspiration from. 'I treasure a leaf from a tree in Nagasaki that survived the atom bomb that was dropped, that ended the war in Japan, World War II.'[27] But she took an even greater treasure from the war, one that stayed in her heart and mind for the rest of her life.

Asked many decades later how she was able to maintain hope, she referred to her wartime experiences. 'It's partly the way I was born, and I think living through World War II – for about a year, it was hopeless,' she said. 'But there was Churchill with his speeches that inspired determination in the British people that we wouldn't be defeated. And against all odds, we weren't. I think living through that gave me this feeling that even when all seems hopeless, don't give up.'[28]

> Did You Know?
>
> Even sixty years after the rationing of World War II ended, Jane continued to live frugally. She would reuse envelopes and stamps and save sachets of sugar and or miniature bottles of drink she came across on her travels.

A Life with Books

The cultural simplicity and global challenges of the era Jane grew up in made her a bookworm, as she disappeared into their pages. There was no television, so books became important to her. She read *Doctor Doolittle* when she was eight and then, two years later, she read *Tarzan and the Apes*. 'I didn't have any female explorers or scientists to look up to but I was inspired by Doctor Dolittle, Tarzan and Mowgli in *The Jungle Book* – all male characters,'[29] she explained. She also enjoyed *The Call of the Wild*, a title that seems almost prescient for Jane.

THE
Story of
Doctor Dolittle
HUGH LOFTING

But it was Doctor Dolittle that had the strongest impact on her life. 'I suppose I was about seven when I met Doctor Dolittle,' she said. On World Book Day in 2016, Jane looked back and remembered this book which meant so much to her and told her supporters about it. It was about an English country doctor living in a place called Puddleby-on-the-Marsh who was taught how to speak to animals by his parrot, Polynesia. But there was one story in particular that made an impact on her: 'The story that really fascinated me was when he took animals from a circus back to Africa on a boat.' It was that story that began her love affair with Africa.[30] Around that time, she had a simple wish: to have a parrot to teach her animal language like Dolittle. In her efforts to communicate with the animal kingdom she even pretended to her friends that she could in fact understand them. Oftentimes she pretended to interpret dogs and cat and birds and they believed her.

She had such a love of the book that, on one occasion, her mother had borrowed the book for

Jane from the library because the family couldn't readily afford to buy books. 'I read it at least twice before it had to go back', remembered Jane. And to her surprise, because she loved the book so much, Danny gave her a copy of it for Christmas in 1944. 'It was one of the most exciting presents I remember – my very own book!' [31] wrote Jane.

In time, she would save up her own few pennies of pocket money and spend them on books. She loved poetry, enjoying the verses of Wilfred Owen, Rupert Brooke, Walter de la Mare, Alfred Noyes and Francis Thompson. She called some of them 'squidgy poets', a reference to the squidgy leather-bound volumes she read. She loved to read by the fire during cold, wet weather.

Jane was able to buy books cheaply at a second-hand bookshop, a place she really loved. And she remembered it well. It was run by an old man called Arturio. 'He would buy lots of books sold from people's libraries. The shop was tiny and the shelves were close together. Little lighting – saving energy for the war effort. It had books higgelty piggelty all over the place, and the old man really didn't know what he had, so you could get great bargains.'[32]

Jane read every book about African animals she could find. *The Miracle of Life* was another book acquired by Danny, who charmingly saved up coupons from cereal packets to get a copy of the science tome. 'It was not a book intended for children, but it was my bible and I spent hours studying and learning from it,' wrote Jane.[33] 'The hefty and dense book went into the history of medicine and the discovery of anaesthetics, and I can still see the pictures and I loved it. I read it, I drew it. I drew the insect mandibles. I really was a naturalist from when I was born.'[34]

Jane enjoyed her time at school, and each year her school held a prize for the best essay on a specific subject. 'To my huge delight (for I wanted to write from a very early age) I won – twice!' wrote Jane. One year, the prize came with a sum of money to use for buying a book. 'I don't remember how much, but it was a fortune to me,' she wrote. She decided to go for a bargain. 'Of course, I went and spent a glorious time in Arturio's'. With her newly acquired riches she was able to choose about twelve books, including poetry books and Samuel Taylor Coleridge's *The Rime of the Ancient Mariner*, illustrated with engravings by Gustave Doré. 'It measured twenty by fifteen inches,' recalled Jane.[35]

Jane loved *The Lord of the Rings* and felt the story was a great way to rouse people from a 'seemingly meaningless life'. As she said in *The Book of Hope*, the force the heroes were up against seemed utterly invincible, but they managed to overcome it. She also saw Tolkien's work as a kind of blueprint for how we survive on our planet with the villains representing all the wickedness in the world, and then the fellowship of the ring representing those willing to fight for good. This strong sense of morals stayed with her throughout her life.

Other books she recommended included *The Wind In the Willows* by Kenneth Grahame, the poems of Thomas Hardy, *All Creatures Great and Small* by James Herriot, *Someone Knows My Name* by Lawrence Hill, *Etre the Cow* by Sean Kenniff, *The No. 1 Ladies' Detective Agency* by Alexander McCall Smith, and *The Chimps of Fauna Sanctuary* by Andrew Westoll.

More recently, Jane also enjoyed reading *What the World Needs Now: Trees!* by Cheryl Rosebush. She described how it 'presents the vital role played by trees to a young audience in a way which will captivate, educate and inspire many to join the global effort to protect forests and plant trees'. When Rosebush discovered that she had Jane's seal of approval, she was thrilled. 'The best thing that could possibly happen with my first book just happened,' she said.[36]

Jane said her favourite place to read was on a plane journey and that she preferred audiobooks, because her eyes were so tired at the end of the day from sitting in front of a screen. What moved her most in a work of literature was, she said, 'the ability to create characters that become absolutely real so that you feel you know them, and which describe events – both current and historical – so that you become immersed in the world that is written about'.

In the years leading up to the Covid pandemic, Jane went on reading marathons, devouring tomes in all sorts of genres. She read books about World War II and the stories of people who worked in the underground in the resistance movement. She read about the Holocaust and the slave trade. She read novels by authors such as Barbara Pym and Graham Greene, and romantic fiction by Rosamunde Pilcher and Mary Wesley. Quite an eclectic mix.

When she was asked which three authors she would invite to a dinner party, Jane struggled to keep the numbers down. The names of William Shakespeare, JRR Tolkien, Jane Austen and Charlotte Brontë rolled straight off her tongue.

Then she wanted John Keats, Lord Byron, Rachel Carson, Charles Dickens and Charles Darwin. 'And, oh, I so want Churchill and, and, and – my dinner party will need a banqueting hall to fit them all in!'

But there were topics she wished authors would write about more, including 'the amazing people and projects around the world that show the resilience of nature, the indomitable human spirit, the power of informed young people', as well as the amazing innovation of scientists fighting climate change.[37]

> Did You Know?
>
> Jane's favourite animal was the dog. 'Dogs have taught me so much and dogs are so faithful, and dogs give unconditional love, and I don't like to think of a world without dogs.'[38] A dog called Rusty, which belonged to a hotel near the Goodall home, became Jane's dear friend when she was a child.

Dreaming of Africa

Jane's reading about Tarzan inspired more than just her hormones, it also gave her a dream for her life. She instantly fell in love with Tarzan, but it also spurred a much deeper desire to go to Africa and live with the animals – just like Tarzan and Jane. She wanted to live there and write books about them.

One day, Vanne took her to the cinema to see her first Tarzan film as a treat. When the curtains drew back to reveal Johnny Weissmuller in the lead role, however, Jane burst into a flood of tears. When she finally managed to compose herself in the cinema's foyer, she told her mother firmly that the man playing Tarzan was absolutely not the *real* Tarzan.

But Jane was not deterred. She told everybody that she wanted to go to Africa, live with wild animals and write books about them. Most people laughed at her, but not her mother Vanne.

This was a crucial moment in Jane's life. 'It was only my mother who supported my dream. "You'll have to work hard, take advantage of opportunities and never give up," she'd tell me. I've shared that message with young people around the world, and so many have thanked me, and said, "You taught me that because you did it, I can do it too."'[39]

Her mother's support was foundational in many ways, including with her education. Jane always did well at school, even though she was busy helping out with the animals at her riding school, where she volunteered to clean harnesses, ride horses and worked on the farm.

Some people say their school days were the happiest days of their life but those times can bring challenges, too. All schools have their bullies and bullying was a problem that Jane thought a lot about during her life. She set her practical mind to work in an attempt to try and detect signs of bullying.

She detected it later in life within her own family. 'One of my sister's grandchildren started out being a little bit of a bully, but we didn't let him,' she said. 'We sat down and explained it to him and told him, how would he like it if people did that to him? He was strong, but he's the sweetest child now and wouldn't hurt a fly.'[40]

★ ★ ★

Jane's school years continued. With her grounding in faith from an early age, Jane began attending church more regularly as a teenager, particularly when her local church appointed a new minister, Trevor Davies. To say she rather took a shine to him might be an understatement. 'He was highly intelligent and his sermons were powerful and thought-provoking,' she wrote.[41] She found herself all the more motivated to attend church with the new vicar around. Trevor Davies not only had an impact on her faith but her philosophy too. He once lent Jane a philosophy book about sensationalism, which is the idea that knowledge originates from the sensory experience, and she wrote a poem to him in response.

But time away from church was most torturous for Jane, so to help her get through the six bleak days between one Sunday and the next, she would make excuses to walk at night past the church and the 'lighted square of his study window, and, with luck, glimpse the top of his head as he wrote his sermons'. She said that she imagined all manner of adventures with him but described it as a platonic infatuation.

Her view of the world was about to expand further, however, and the young Jane needed all the support and belief she could muster. Inequality between men and women was so strong at the time that Jane didn't even dare dream of what she wanted, without editing her dreams. 'When I was a little girl, I used to dream as a man, because I wanted to do things that women didn't do back then such as traveling to Africa, living with wild animals and writing books.'[42] But she continued to

be ambitious despite having no female role models in her field.

> Did You Know?
>
> When asked by *The Times* newspaper if she'd prefer a night at the Ritz or a night under the stars, Jane chose a night under the stars.

Breaking the Mould

When Jane left school, there wasn't enough money to send her to university so, as she told *The Telegraph*, 'I took a boring old secretarial course and got a job in London'.

Jane's ambitions were unorthodox compared to those of other women. In the 1950s, of course young women had exciting dreams, but many of them were the same. 'Most girls were really interested in becoming air hostesses; it was the big thing in those days,' she said. 'You had to be super-qualified to be an air hostess in the early days; you had to know something about nursing, medicine, speak several languages. You had to be beautiful as well as all those things.'[43] A friend once suggested that Jane herself could become an air hostess, but she vehemently refused the idea. Her mother used to call them 'gloried waitresses', and she agreed wholeheartedly.

There were many expectations for Jane as a young woman. Writing in *Time*, she remembered how her paternal uncle, Sir Michael Spens, son of Lord Patrick Spens, wanted to present her at court as a debutante during the season of dances and balls. She saw this as a kind of marriage market and completely absurd. Nevertheless, she was obliged to attend. 'I had to humour Michael, and so I lined up in Buckingham Palace to shake hands with the Queen. I remember being surrounded by girls who said to me, "Don't you dream of being a lady-in-waiting?" I replied, "Absolutely not – I want to live among wild animals." They recoiled in horror. They thought I was very weird, but then I thought they were very weird, too.'[44]

But Jane had bigger plans of course and her African dream was about to come true. She was going to Kenya to visit a friend whose family had a farm near Nairobi in Kenya. She wouldn't be flying there though. 'Of course, there were no 747s or package tours in those days; it really was the dark continent,' she said.[45] There were no affordable planes going back and forth in those days, so she travelled to Africa by boat.

How nearly it all went wrong! She was standing on the dock ready to sail on the *Kenya Castle* in March 1957 when she realized that her passport was missing. She was devastated. She'd saved for two years to pay for her journey to Kenya, taking on a range of jobs including shifts at the local post office, waitressing and secretarial work. Now, it seemed her trip was in danger. How had she lost the passport? She'd spent a few days in London, buying supplies for the trip at Peter Jones, the department store on Kings Road where, as a toddler, she had so unsettled the doorman. But at the last minute, all her preparations seemed to have gone to waste.

Luckily, however, someone had found her passport and noticed an itinerary from Cook's, the travel agency, stored inside. They delivered the passport to Cook's office and an office worker rushed it to her as she stood on the dock. This was a stroke of luck which perhaps hinted at divine support for her plan. 'Incredible, amazing,' Jane remarked, looking back on that moment.

⋆ ⋆ ⋆

Her journey on the *Kenya Castle* would take nearly a month but within twenty-four hours, many of the passengers were deep into terrible sea sickness. While onboard, she wrote a letter to her family saying that to avoid seasickness, she set herself at close as possible to the front of the ship. She took the opportunity to connect with people and made friends with other passengers, including an engineer, a governess and a man who volunteered at a leper colony.

She also connected with nature and loved how the sea changed colour as the bow rose and fell. 'The sea is dark inky blue, then it rises up a clear transparent blue green, and then it breaks in white and sky-blue foam,' she wrote in the letter. 'But best of all, some of this foam is forced back under the wave from which it broke, and this spreads out under the surface like the palest blue milk, all soft and hazy at the edge.'[46]

She read Monica Dickens' *One Pair of Hands* during the journey, a book she would later re-read many times when she caught malaria in Africa.[47]

The Suez Canal was closed because of a war on the Sinai Peninsula, so the *Kenya Castle* took the longer route around the Cape of Good Hope. But when Jane first set foot on African soil in Cape Town, she had a rude awakening. Her initial love for the place was diminished when she asked some locals what a sign written in Afrikaans meant. They told her it said, 'White people only'. This went against Jane's principles. She insisted that such segregation went against her upbringing as her grandfather was an inspirational Congregational minister who showed kindness to people from other cultures. She remembered him fondly and noted that they never judged people by the colour of their skin, or their language and religion. They were human beings and should be treated as such. Thankfully, her experience in Kenya was much better than the one in Cape Town.

It was a tough start but soon the ship reached Mombasa, on the Indian Ocean, and Jane found the Africa of her dreams with animals all around her. She could hardly believe her eyes.

Naturally, Jane's earliest impressions of Africa continued to involve animals. 'The very first morning there was a fresh leopard track on the farm and I saw an aardvark on the road – I've never seen that since,' she said. It was a revelation.

'Seeing a giraffe close up . . . however much you know giraffes, to see one in the wild for the first time feels prehistoric.'[48]

Soon she saw a lion for the first time, a moment she would never forget. 'I sensed something behind me – and looking round saw, about three hundred yards away, a young male lion, probably around two years old, full grown, but with his mane just sprouting from his shoulders,' she wrote. 'He was standing and staring at us. He had almost certainly never seen white women, and he was curious. I had no sense of fear – just excitement.'[49] There would be plenty more excitement to come.

★ ★ ★

Through her friends, Jane met Louis Leakey, a Kenyan-born paleoanthropologist who became one of the most celebrated scientists of the twentieth century. This was a huge fork in the road for Jane's life. Initially, Louis gave her a job as an assistant secretary at his museum. This proved quite the education for Jane. 'The staff all were keen naturalists full of enthusiasm and were happy to share some of their boundless knowledge with me,' she wrote. It was a somewhat dreary office job but she snapped up the opportunity because she didn't want to overstay her welcome working at her friend farm.

When she was on the small island of Lolui in Lake Victoria, Jane had a hair-raising encounter with a local crocodile poacher. At first, she thought an animal was following her but she soon realized it was a man clad only in a loincloth and with a spear in one hand. She stepped into a tunnel that a hippopotamus had made for grazing and asked of the man, 'Jambo – how are you?' He raised his spear, lowered it and then began speaking angrily to her. She thought he was threatening to kill her if he ever saw her again.

But her brief time on Lolui proved a good practice run for what was to come, and opened her eyes to the way humans interact with animals.

'The short trip taught me a good deal about such things as note-taking in the field, the sort of clothes to wear, the movements a wild monkey will tolerate in a human observer and those it will not,' she wrote.[50]

Leakey wanted some insights into chimpanzee ethology and asked Jane to help. He felt that by studying man's closest relatives, he could better understand early human behaviour, something the fossil record could not tell him. 'I was really lucky,' she said, 'because Louis Leakey believed that women would make better observers in the field than men. He thought that they would be more patient.' But Jane didn't even know what ethology was. 'I had to wait quite a while before I realized it simply meant studying behaviour.'[51]

While Leakey made plans for a research expedition and applied for the necessary permissions, Jane returned to England in December 1958 and began work in Granada Television's film library, which was housed inside London Zoo.

There she could study the behaviour of primates while saving money to fund her expedition.

In May 1960, Jane heard that Leakey had finally secured funding for the expedition and she boarded a plane for Nairobi.

Chapter Two

Dr Jane

1960–1985

'People often assume I'm stern and serious: Dr Jane Goodall PhD DBE. They're surprised I've got a wicked sense of humour.'

—Jane Goodall in an interview with *The Guardian*[1]

Life in Gombe

In July 1960, Jane boarded a boat, much smaller than the *Kenya Castle*, and for a much shorter journey. After a few hours sailing over Lake Tanganyika, she stepped onto the pebbly beach at Gombe, and into her new life in Tanzania. That new life in Gombe would be challenging: she recalled how aloneness became a way of life for her.

At that time, the total population of chimps in was approximately one million. Just one hundred or so lived in the Gombe reserve.

To adhere to the colonial safety guidelines of the time, her mother Vanne joined her as a chaperone. 'Initially I wasn't allowed to be on my own,' she told the BBC. 'The British government as it then was said, "No, this is absolutely almost amoral for a young girl to go out in the bush." So, I had to choose a companion, and my mother came with me for three months.'[2]

They slept in a former army camping tent. During her first months in Gombe Park, Tanzania, she contracted malaria thirty to forty times. But she put up with the suffering because she had a mighty ambition. 'The primary aim of my field study was to discover as much as possible about the way of life of the chimpanzee before it is too late – before encroachments of civilization crowd out, forever, all non-human competitors,' she wrote in the August 1963 issue of *National Geographic*. 'Knowledge of social traditions and culture of such an animal, studied under natural conditions, could throw new light on the growth and spread of early human cultures.'[3]

It continued to be simple living and high thinking in their basic tent. 'If you wanted air to come in, you just rolled up the sides and tied them with tape,' she told *The Guardian*. 'Well, the air came in, but the spiders, scorpions and snakes came in as well.'[4] It was easy to become preoccupied with domestic living so Jane and

Vanne hired a cook to ensure that Jane had plenty of time to work.

Her kit was simple, too. She carried with her a notebook along with a pair of binoculars that were second hand. At first, she was banned from roaming too far on her own, but eventually, as she learned the forest trails and got accustomed to the dense terrain, 'the authorities decided, well, I was crazy and I was okay',[5] she said.

Eventually Jane was able to start observing the animals she wanted to study. But this had its challenges. 'And of course, the first problem was that the chimps ran away as soon as they saw me. They'd never seen anything like this white ape before.'[6] She wanted to observe the chimpanzees up close and developed several tactics to make this prospect more likely. 'I wore the same-coloured clothes every day and I think the most important thing was I never pushed it,' she said. 'I never tried to get too close. I would wait by a fruiting tree,

where I knew the chimpanzees were coming, and when they left, I didn't follow them. Not to start with, because I felt that was pushing my luck. So gradually they came to accept that I was harmless.'[7]

> Did You Know?
>
> When she was observing the chimpanzees in Gombe, Jane either wore low-top canvas sneakers or went barefoot.

A New Discovery

In October 1960, Jane watched as a chimpanzee bent a twig, stripped off its leaves, and used it to 'fish' termites from their nest. She was the first to discover that the ability to use tools was not uniquely human. This moment rewrote our understanding of animals and changed Jane's own life forever.

In 1947, Kenneth Oakley, a physical anthropologist and palaeontologist, set out what was then the consensus, during a conference held at the Natural History Museum in London. 'It is in making tools that man is unique,' wrote Oakley. 'The shaping of sticks and stones to particular uses was the first recognizably human activity,' he noted.[8]

It is hard to overstate how important Jane's discovery was. Before it, 'many people saw chimps as entertaining curiosities who featured in zoos and circuses – sometimes dressed as mini-humans for laughs – but lacking their own culture', explained the *Financial Times*.[9]

After Jane's termite moment, the understanding of scientists about the difference between humanity and the rest of the animal kingdom would never be the same again. As Leakey wrote, 'Now we must redefine tool, redefine Man, or accept chimpanzees as human.' Jane's project was supposed to end

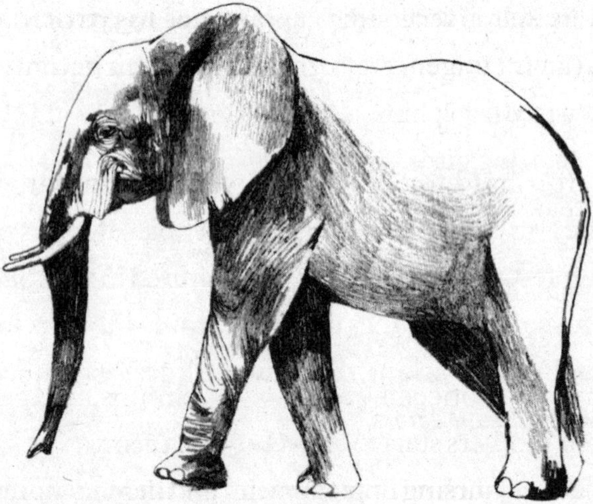

within months, but her discovery led to renewed support and more research.

Did You Know?

As well as venerating chimps, Jane has praised the intelligence of other species, including 'whales, dolphins, elephants and lions, all these amazing birds, many of whom perform better than chimps'.[10]

Animal Behaviour

Jane also noticed how, as infant chimps mature, their mothers start to actively wean their young by rejecting nursing opportunities and denying them attempts to hitch a ride on their backs. At the same time, they expose their infants to more and more social interactions.

Only later, in 2019, a study published in the journal *PNAS* (the *Proceedings of the National*

Academy of Sciences) weaved the tool and parenting observations together, when it revealed that chimp mothers in the Republic of Congo were teaching their infants how to fish for termites by giving them their own stick rods as hand-me-downs.

Jane loved observing the intimacy of the family bonds and how each animal's individuality would influence their behaviour. 'In chimp society, a female can be mated by all the males, or she can be led away and kept by one, and the males have very close bonds,' she told the BBC's *Wogan* show. 'They patrol the boundary of the community territory, they keep strangers out, they bring young new-blood females in, and all of them act as nice, tolerant, gentle, protective fathers to all the infants inside that community.' Jane sat silently observing the chimpanzees, absolutely fascinated by what she witnessed. She noticed how familiar their family bonds and their non-verbal communication were. 'If chimps meet after a separation, they hold hands, they embrace, they kiss,' she said, asking herself whether this raised 'new questions about the way that we are bringing up our children in the West'.

Jane believed that if a parent left a child crying at night, or for long hours in a playpen, or if they left a child at a daycare centre with a constant turnover of people, they may end up with a child that is highly intelligent. But the observation of chimps told a different story. From her research there was the suggestion that a child would struggle to make connections with other people if they'd had a difficult upbringing. It was hugely important.

Oftentimes, the chimpanzees she was observing would retreat to a waterfall, where they would perform ritual dances, before sitting and quietly contemplating the water, reaching towards understanding. Jane imagined them thinking, 'What is this stuff that's always coming and it's always going but it's always here? The sun, the stars . . . what are they? What do they mean?'[11]

Jane's approach to listing the animals was groundbreaking. 'When I started out, I was told animals needed numbers not names, that mind, personality and emotion were unique to humanity. To me, this was so obviously not the case. A fact anyone with a pet could attest to.'[12]

This would also be true when Jane completed her PhD. At Cambridge, she set herself apart from custom by naming the animals in her studies of primates instead of merely assigning each a number. She was known for her curious thesis in which she referred to the individual chimps by pet names such as David Greybeard (whom she first saw using tools) and Flo (the matriarch of the troop).

'When, in the early 1960s, I brazenly used such words as "childhood", "adolescence", "motivation", "excitement" and "mood", I was much criticized. Even worse was my crime of suggesting that chimpanzees had "personalities". I was ascribing human characteristics to non-human animals and was thus guilty of that worst of ethological sins – anthropomorphism. But to my dismay, I was quickly told that I had done my study all wrong,' she told *Time*. She was advised that she should have numbered the chimps rather than given them names and that she shouldn't talk about their personalities, minds or emotions as those features were unique to humans and there is a difference between humans and all other animals.

'That way of thinking, of course, makes it easier to treat animals as things rather than sentient and sapient beings able to experience joy, fear, despair and pain,' she said in the *Time* interview. 'Easier to work in a factory farm or medical research laboratory and for us to enjoy the sport of trophy hunting.'

Jane understood the true nature of animals from Rusty, her pet dog and childhood teacher. 'So I knew that in this respect the Cambridge professors were wrong – as does everyone who has shared their life in a meaningful way with a dog or a horse or a hamster or a bird.'

One of the major differences to Jane's work is that she didn't come from a scientific background. She wrote in *Science* 'As I had not had an undergraduate science education, I did not realize that animals were not supposed to have personalities, or to think, or to feel emotions or pain . . . I did not realize that it was unscientific to discuss behavior in terms of motivation or purpose. It was not respectable, in scientific circles, to talk about animal personality. That was something reserved for humans.' [13] But Jane continued to challenge expectations.

Did You Know?

While many people think chimps would be Jane's favourite animal, it was actually dogs. 'Chimps are way too human. I didn't even think of them as animals. They're just beings.'

The Scientific Community

As she began to rub shoulders with scientists, Jane found that her spiritual beliefs didn't always go down well. She was surprised to find so many scientists felt that science and religion were incompatible and that many scientists were atheists or agnostics.

Nevertheless, her spiritual consciousness was developing. St Francis of Assisi was a big influence on Jane. He was an Italian mystic, poet and Catholic friar who was born in 1181. He was associated with the patronage of animals and the environment so it should be no surprise that he became so significant to Jane. 'He was a mystic who lived a simple life, and he not only helped the poor, but was a lover of nature and animals,' she said in 2003. St Francis saw God reflected in the natural world just like Jane. 'When I was on my own in the rainforest of Gombe, where I studied chimpanzees for years, I became part of nature and I felt such a strong connection with the great spiritual power which with my Christian upbringing I would call God,' she said.

'I was awed by the wonder of nature and felt a close connection not only with the animals but with the whole environment. Like St Francis, I would greet familiar trees and the streams and the peak from which I used to watch the chimps and I felt awe and wonder as I lay at night looking up at the stars sensing the infinity of the universe.' [14]

When Pope Francis died in 2025, Jane made a connection between him and St Francis. 'St Francis of Assisi is for me a truly saintly human being, one who lived a simple life, and cared for nature and animals as well as those despised or shunned by the society he lived in', she wrote. 'Like him, Pope Francis did all he could for such people, and even blessed the marriage of gay couples.' [15] It seems clear that Jane's spirituality was never far from her scientific curiosity about the world.

Did You Know?

Girls in Action, a programme run by the Jane Goodall Institute, empowers girls in communities near chimpanzee habitats. Through its work, it creates sustainable livelihoods, which in turn reduces the tendency of destructive practices, benefiting both local people and chimpanzees alike.

But the scientific community presented other challenges for Jane. As Jane and her work became better known, she was confronted with some patronizing and sexist views of women. A headline for an article about her work focused on her appearance, saying, 'Comely Miss Spends her Time Eyeing Apes'.

More than one reporter wrote about her legs. But as Jane often did, she looked on the bright side. She explained that she wasn't too troubled by this – 'If my legs helped me to get publicity for the chimps, well, that was useful.'[16]

But the sexist tone of her media coverage continued. When she later went to America to give a few talks there were some 'rather sensational articles, emphasizing my blond hair and referring to my legs', she told *Time*. Although some scientists discredited her observations because of this, she wasn't bothered so long as she got the funding to return to Gombe and continue her work. 'I had never wanted to be a scientist anyway, as women didn't have such careers in those days,' she said. 'I just wanted to be a naturalist.'

Perhaps because of their shared experience as women in the scientific community, Rachel Carson, the ecologist and conservationist, was a big influence on Jane. In the 1960s, Carson's book *Silent Spring* was published and Jane was inspired by her courage in battling with pharmaceutical companies, the government and scientists about the danger to the environment of DDT, the insecticide that proved to have harmful effects on wildlife.[17]

Jane was still doing her research around this time but she wasn't overly concerned with securing her PhD because she had other priorities. While she described it as something 'nice to have', for her, the research took primary importance. Her focus was on starting a research station that was fully funded and her focus was on making it happen whether she had a PhD or not. But ultimately, she did identify an advantage from gaining those three letters, which she achieved in 1965: 'When I'd done that, I could stand up and talk to a scientist in a white coat,' she explained.[18]

Following Jane's significant contribution to the scientific community, the Jane Goodall Institute, a non-profit wildlife and environmental conservation organization, was founded in 1977. She co-founded the Institute with Genevieve di San Faustino. Known as 'Genie', di San Faustino met Jane during a trip to Africa. She became the founding President of the Jane Goodall Institute and it went on to run a number of projects that are still ongoing today.

> Did You Know?
>
> The Senegal Chimp Project is one of the Jane Goodall Institute's proudest projects. It uses Jane's Tacare approach, which recognizes that protecting wildlife and supporting local people must go hand in hand.

Chimpanzee Observations

Jane adored and treasured her memories of watching the chimps care for each other. 'I remember a little three-year-old male chimp called Mel who was orphaned after his mother died,' she told *National Geographic*. 'Mel was just beginning to eat solid foods, and so he'd reached an age where he could theoretically survive without his mother. Unfortunately, his survival seemed unlikely as he didn't have an older brother or sister to care for him – which is what would normally happen.'

But then something surprising happened. 'To our amazement, a twelve-year-old unrelated male called Spindle adopted him! He carried him around on his back, rescued him from difficult situations, reached out and took him into his nest at night, shared his food with him. Spindle saved the little orphan's life!'

This was the first time that Jane had witnessed this behaviour with unrelated chimps, and she found it 'very moving because Spindle had just lost his own mother, so it was almost like this little infant had helped him get over his grief'.[19] Jane saw this as a demonstration of altruism that had been thought to be beyond the capacity of animals.

Jane's affection for the chimps was misunderstood by many but she remained adamant in her belief that the chimps should be viewed differently. 'You would fall head over heels in love with all my darlings,' she wrote to Louis Leakey. 'I shall come back here time and time again until the problems that remain are hardly worth mentioning again.'[20]

The criticism, however, continued. Jane could recall a time she'd been dismissed for not being scientific enough. One such critic was Sir Solly Zuckerman, an anatomist who had studied monkeys in Africa, and became secretary of the Zoological Society of London (ZSL) and chief science adviser to the Ministry of Defence. He had talked down to her after she had given a talk at the ZSL in April 1962.

'There are those who are here and who prefer anecdote – and what I must confess I regard as sometimes unbounded speculation,' he said. 'In scientific work it is far safer to base one's major conclusions and generalizations on a concordant and large body of data.'

Jane wasn't at all surprised by his tone. The previous year, she'd planned to use a press conference at London Zoo to call for an improvement in the conditions of the captive chimps there. The chimps' cages were bare, with cement floor that got incredibly hot which was completely unacceptable to Jane. But she was warned that Zuckerman would not appreciate this approach as it would be seen as a criticism of his leadership. So instead, she acted behind the scenes. She quietly suggested several simple changes to the chimps' enclosure. 'What I learned then is: don't let people lose face, don't try to do something publicly until you've tried every which way to do it quietly. I've found that so helpful to me.'[21]

Zuckerman continued to be defensive and wary. In a brief letter to the ethologist Desmond Morris, he wrote of his own anxiety, stirred by Jane's conference presentation, 'lest a subject which has been usually marked by unscientific treatment should continue in the unscientific shadows because of glamour'.[22]

Jane had much to overcome during her lifetime, but after she died, the ZSL Chief Executive Matthew Gould attempted to set the record straight. 'Some members of the scientific community, including – I am ashamed to say – a scientist from ZSL, were critical, dismissing her work as "anecdote and . . . speculation" based on "contradictory and isolated observations that contributed little to science". But history, of course, proved the critics wrong.'[23]

Few female readers will be surprised to learn that, when the improvements were eventually made to the chimp enclosure at London Zoo, Zuckerman took the credit for them. 'I don't mind two hoots as long as it gets done,' Goodall told *The Guardian*.[24]

Jane was always keen to share the credit for any breakthroughs she made. She didn't just share it with other people – she would share it with other species and often pointed out that it was the chimpanzees themselves who changed human understanding. According to her, they played an important role in helping her change people's perceptions and helped people see humanity as a part of the animal kingdom rather than something separate from it.

Research has suggested that chimpanzees are incredibly genetically close to humans, sharing about 98.6 per cent of our DNA. As Jane explained, 'Behaviour we see in man today and chimp today was probably in that common ancestor, and therefore we can imagine Stone Age people having long friendly relationships between family members and using little twigs to feed and embracing one another. I like to think of that.' This is the reason why chimps weren't Jane's favourite animal – because they are so like us humans.

Humans can learn lessons from chimps, she believed, and there were separate lessons for women and men. For modern Western women, they can learn from chimpanzees about how a positive experience in the early years of a child's life can have a big impact on their adulthood. As for men, there was a different lesson: 'Chimpanzee males can be excellent caregivers to infants,' she said. 'Sometimes it's a brother, which makes sense, but sometimes it's an adult male who cares for an orphaned infant. Within the human male there is this parental instinct, if we accept that we've inherited a lot of these similar characteristics from a common ancestor.[25]

Jane was always keen to show the comparison between humans and chimps. 'Perhaps the most important thing we've learned at Gombe is how similar we are to these creatures, with whom we share between 95 and 98 percent of our DNA. As we watch their numbers dwindle and their forests fall, their legacy becomes as clear as a Gombe stream: as they go, so, one day, may we.'[26]

Did You Know?

Jane's first grant to fund her research was $1,400 and came from the National Geographic Society.

A New Adventure

In 1964, Jane married Hugo van Lawick, a Dutch photographer. They had met when *National Geographic* sent van Lawick to document her research in Africa, a prospect she wasn't too keen on initially.

'I really didn't want him to come,' she later told the podcast Call Her Daddy. 'I hadn't met him because I just wanted to be there with the chimps, you know. I didn't want anybody and I was afraid they'd be scared of him and, you know, all my hard work would be undone.'

But she soon realized that van Lawick loved animals and always wanted to be out there with them. He was simply using photography as a route to that end. 'We got on fine,' she explained. 'It was thanks to his photos and film that everything I was saying about the chimps was corroborated.' Previously, she felt she had a love affair with her work and with the chimps but then Hugo came along and it all worked out. Even so, the run up to their marriage truly stressed out Jane, as she explained in a letter to her childhood friend, Sally Cary: 'You can't imagine the cables and express letters that went whizzing – and still whiz – between here and Africa, Africa and Holland, Holland and here. My goodness.'[27] Jane described the preparations as 'such horrors' and described what a muddle she was in and exhausted in the extreme. But once the wedding day came, everything seemed to fall into place. She wore a white wedding dress which she found superb and once the day was all over, she and Hugo agreed that they had never been to a wedding they'd enjoyed more.[28]

Following her marriage, Jane took on a new name. Having been born Valerie Jane Morris-Goodall, then becoming known as Jane Goodall, she was now Baroness Jane van Lawick-Goodall.

> Did You Know?
>
> Jane sometimes spotted very mysterious creatures during her expeditions. On more than one occasion in the forest, Jane saw a bird 'the colour of an English fox' which she believed has never been officially identified.

Three years later, Jane and her husband had a son – Hugo Eric Louis. Jane loved becoming a mother. She later told *The Guardian* that her happiest moments were 'when I arrived at Gombe for the first time and when I had a baby'.[29]

She found a hospital in Nairobi where mothers were allowed to keep their babies with them right from the moment they were born. The hospital was a 'darling Catholic one', she said, and the sister there seemed to get that 'for someone who studied chimpanzee infants, it was most desirable that she be able to study her own'.[30]

Jane went into labour at 2am and arrived at the hospital at 4am. The baby finally appeared at 9.45am. As Jane, who had no anaesthetic, described to a friend, the first part of her labour went quickly but then the second half was much slower. By the end everyone was surprised she had enough energy to finish the job!

The issue was that Jane had, she was told, a lazy uterus and her baby had a large head, which resulted in 'thousands of stitches'. To add to her displeasure, the hospital went back on its promise to let her keep the baby with her for his first days.

But Jane was well prepared for this new adventure: she said her chimpanzee research had helped prepare her for parenthood. 'The most important thing is support,' she told *SheKnows*. 'You need to support your child in what they want to do, they might change their mind but don't try and impose what you want your child to do on them, just support them.'

'The chimpanzees have an extremely close bond between mother and child,' she told *People*. 'The mother is constantly with the child, and I raised Grub this way. I never left him for a full day until he was three years old.'

Grub's earliest years were spent at Gombe. Mindful of the risk that the chimps could pose, Jane built a protective cage for him when he was a baby. 'But you could stand upright and walk across it,' she told Fox News. 'He couldn't even crawl. So it was almost like a giant cot.'

'The point was that when he first went to England he wasn't at boarding school,' said Goodall. She was struggling to juggle the demands of her career and motherhood, so when he reached school age she sent him to live with her mother, while she carried on her work at Gombe. 'He wasn't at boarding school, he was with mum, so it was like an extended family . . . we had every holiday together . . . and the rest of the time he was with mum, and it was almost like an extension of myself,' she told *People*.

But sadly, her marriage to van Lawick 'ended gradually'. He was sent to make films about the Serengeti, and Goodall couldn't leave Gombe. She remembered, 'I had to stay . . . I couldn't leave Gombe, and so it slowly drifted apart. And it was sad.' But she concluded that they did the right thing by ending their marriage, because it was inevitable. She believed the experience had been helpful for Hugo too because he also became a well-known name and saw his own rise to fame.

Jane was never much of a one for crying, but marital problems were enough to set her off. 'I haven't cried properly since 1969,' she revealed in 2023. 'TV and film might leave me misty-eyed, but the last time I truly sobbed was when I accepted my first marriage wasn't working.'[31] Their son was only eight when the marriage ended. 'He survived it okay,' she recalled. 'It was sad, but I think it was better.'

⋆ ⋆ ⋆

In 1975, she would marry again. This time to Tanzania's Director of National Parks, Derek Bryceson, who was also a member of the country's national assembly. As with her first husband, Jane hadn't wanted to meet Derek initially. This time, Jane was scared to meet him, because she had heard he was mean and unsympathetic, as she told *People* magazine.

But they met and found happiness together – particularly in solitude. They enjoyed dining alone, and Bryceson said that his ideal life would be to 'stay all year at Gombe, by the clear lake – far away from the city.'

They lived in the same house that she had lived in with her previous husband. Although the house had a door, the windows were made of chicken wire, to keep animals out while still welcoming in as much of Gombe's atmosphere as possible. The set-up was different, but reminiscent of the tents she lived in when she had first arrived in Africa.

But this marriage wouldn't last either because just five years after they wed, Bryceson passed away. 'He got this horrible cancer. That was the end,' she said. 'I came to England to mourn, then returned to Tanzania spending days alone in the forest,' she told *The Guardian*. 'Out in nature grief dissipated. Now I love to think of life after death; exploring that unknown will be my next great adventure.'[32]

Jane never married again because, she told *People* magazine, she 'didn't meet the right person, I suppose, or potentially the right person'. She added

that she had lots of men friends and lots of women friends too, so her life was complete and she didn't need a husband.

Not that she was lacking in opportunities, according to her friend Rick Barongi. 'She had many admirers and even proposals', he said. 'But Jane felt she had a more important calling in life.'[33]

A Change of Heart

For much of her life, Jane didn't eat meat. She became a vegetarian at the end of the 1960s and vegan during the Covid pandemic, when she realized that egg and dairy production are also cruel.

After becoming a vegetarian, Jane wrote to a colleague who was organizing a spring fundraising tour, about her new dietary needs. 'Sue, when you're talking with people I'm going to be staying with, or who are organizing my visits, could you please announce that I utterly will not eat animals' flesh or battery chicken eggs. Absolutely not.'[34]

Initially, she continued to eat fish, partly because Grub enjoyed catching fish. 'I'll have to go on hoping, for a while, that it's not as bad for them,' she wrote. And she reasoned that fish, at least, had a much freer life before they were eaten.

She said she had more energy after she stopped eating meat. 'The moment I stopped eating meat I felt lighter,' she revealed in 2010. 'All I know is that when I stopped eating meat, I just felt lighter and had more energy. My body wasn't wasting time trying to cope with the toxins that the animals were trying to get rid of when you eat them.'[35]

There were other reasons for her tireless energy and passion, she felt, but she was never entirely sure what those reasons were. 'People are always asking me that,' she said. 'Is it that I have grandchildren and I'm so upset about what we've done to their future? Is it that I love the wilderness and I'm so upset to see it disappearing? Is it because I've lived long enough to understand the horrors of things like nuclear war and chemical spills? I don't know.'[36]

Jane's concern for animal welfare continued to be a top priority throughout her life. She was deeply saddened by animal experimentation, which has seen so many billions of animals suffer and die in laboratories. 'The chimpanzee is only one of the many species threatened with extinction in the wild; but he is, after all, our closest living relative and it would be tragic if when our grandchildren are grown the chimpanzee exists only in the zoo and the laboratory.'[37]

She wasn't completely opposed to zoos, however. 'If you had a really good zoo with space and food and things to do, I'd probably choose to be there if I were a chimpanzee,' she said. 'People get very confrontational about their views. I try to back off and think what would a chimpanzee want?'[38]

Nevertheless, if animals were to be exploited in labs, she had a string of conditions. In her book, *In the Shadow of Man*, she describes how the chimp should be treated with the utmost decency like a guest in one's home. She said that he should have a large living area with companions and plenty of things to keep him entertained, as well as being well fed. And there was another stipulation: 'They should stop being sold as pets; our closest living relatives can be bought and sold like slaves.'[39]

Her heart was always with her animal friends and she was a strong advocate for them when anything threatened their way of life, like the development of agriculture and forestry practices were a particular concern to her. 'The least I can do is speak out for those who cannot speak for themselves,' she is known to have said of her support of and love of animals. But while Jane was

a strong advocate for the natural world, there was a darker side she had yet to encounter.

> Did You Know?
>
> The Jane Goodall Institute published a cookbook entitled *The Jane Goodall Institute #EatMeatless*. The charity Veganuary listed the book as number one on its list of Best Vegan Cookbooks.

The Gombe Chimpanzee War

In 1970, Jane was appointed to a faculty at Stanford University. There was no naivety or childlike romance to her studies. She was truthful. After ten years, her work revealed that although chimps were 'very like us in their friendly ways, they're also like us in the fact they can become very aggressive', she said. 'We found that under certain situations, there can be cannibalism and also an inter-community interaction that in some way is like a primitive form of human warfare.'[40]

The Gombe Chimpanzee War, also known as the Four-Year War, was a violent conflict between two communities of chimpanzees in Gombe, which Jane witnessed firsthand. It devastated her. 'The four years from 1974 through 1977 were the darkest in Gombe's history, and some of the most intellectually and emotionally challenging years of my life,' she wrote in *Reason for Hope*, adding that her peaceful way of life was completely upended by the war. As well as the heartache of the violence, in her personal life at the time, she was contending with her own divorce that had its own emotional weight.

The sheer violence between the chimpanzees 'changed forever my view of chimpanzee nature', she wrote. For ten years, she'd believed that the Gombe chimpanzees were mostly 'rather nicer than human beings', but she suddenly realized they could be brutal and that they had a dark side to their nature. She would wake up in the night with horrific pictures of violence in her mind.

Again, she showed humility and vision when she suggested that humans could learn from chimpanzees. 'One of the things that strikes me is how important it is in their society to very quickly make friends again after an aggressive incident. Particularly obvious in captive groups when they can't just go wandering off on their own, but we see it in the wild too.

'Take an adolescent male, terrified of this male, the big male has distracted him. And even though he's terrified, that youngster will come up and make some kind of submissive response to that, the aggressor reacts, then pats him, kisses him or hugs him. And you just see social harmony instantly restored. And I think that's something that we can learn about.'[41]

Jane wasn't without fear but she also understood her subject matter. 'Sometimes I was scared because they are about ten times stronger than we are,' she said. 'But, fortunately, they are not really aggressive toward us. They respect us, we respect them. Nobody's ever been really hurt in the wild. In captivity, yes, because they don't necessarily like the people when they are in captivity.'[42]

But she was always ready to see the light as much as the shade. 'Chimps have a sense of humour,' she said. 'So you're trailing a vine around a tree and your little brother is following, and every time he's going to grab it, you jerk it forward. After a bit, he starts to cry, and you start to laugh. That's very funny for them. At that level, we're the same.'[43]

When Jane brought all of her findings together, she realized that her lack of scientific background was not necessarily a disadvantage, but could be viewed as an advantage. 'You see, the fortunate thing was I didn't have the scientific education so I went ahead and described the obvious,' she said.[44]

Just as she didn't think religion and science were necessarily opposed, she also thought empathy and research did not need to be separated. 'I was also told that scientists must be coldly objective and never show empathy for their subjects,' she told *Time*. 'But you can make observations that are absolutely scientifically accurate even while having empathy for the being you are studying. In fact, it can sometimes provide an intuition about the meaning of a certain behaviour. You can then test your intuition with scientific rigor.'

> Did You Know?
>
> Jane's first book-length study, *In the Shadow of Man* (1971), has been translated into forty-eight languages.

Significant Ideas

Wherever Jane was in the world, she always loved to read. An old friend of hers, Hugh Caldwell, gave her a book called *Human Destiny*, which was written in 1937 by the French doctor-turned-philosopher

Lecomte du Noüy. In it, the author argues for a teleological view of evolution, proposing that human existence is not mere chance but guided by a purpose. Strict materialism is invalid, wrote du Noüy, and moral and spiritual evolution is the next necessary step for mankind.

The book had quite an impact on Jane and fuelled that sense of hope that would define her, as well as her sense of spiritualism, which grew throughout her life. She cited the book as a point of fascination for her and how it influenced her thinking over the dark time in Gombe. While she was familiar with the physical evolution of a species, this was the first time she considered a moral evolution. If humans had the ability to rid themselves of immoral attributes found in aggression and war-mongering, then perhaps chimpanzees too could learn to adapt in this way. Typical to her outlook on the natural world, these ideas weren't exclusive for humankind; as Jane observed the chimps she saw that a cultural evolution was possible. Here she began to think about her seemingly hopeless situation in a new way.

These foundational ideas drove Jane's work forward as she became more engaged in her moral ambition.

Chapter Three

Taking Up the Fight

1986–1999

'I feel that all of us are put on this
planet with a role to play.'

—Jane Goodall

Opened Eyes

During the 1980s, Jane was developing yet more steeliness and determination as she learned even more about the plight of animals in laboratories. Two days after Christmas 1986, she and her family watched an undercover video shot at an American bioresearch laboratory, which used chimpanzees for experiments. The footage was harrowing. 'We all sat watching the tape and we are all shattered,' she wrote. 'Afterward, we couldn't speak for a while.'[1] She said later that she had closed her eyes for too long on the issue, but 'now they have been opened so widely that it is hard for me to sleep at night'.

In 1987, she was invited to take a tour of an animal research lab. Any hope that the tour had won her over and she would write a letter declaring her endorsement was quickly dispelled when her guide declared, 'Jane, at least you will agree that these chimpanzees are well cared for'. Wiping tears from her face, Jane replied that she refused to write a letter.

She described seeing the plight of chimpanzees in labs as her 'Damascus moment' because it was horrendous for her. 'Seeing our closest relatives, who can live up to – well, more than sixty years – in five foot by five foot medical research labs, surrounded by iron bars, totally alone, nothing to do, just because their bodies are so like ours that we share 98.6 percent of our DNA.'[2]

After that experience, Jane knew that she needed to do more to help. 'It was like I went as a scientist, and I left as a – I suppose you'd call me an activist or something like that. Just happened. I knew I had to do something.'[3]

The year before, she had attended a gathering of primatologists in Chicago. As the conference wore on, she noticed a common theme running through the discussions. 'Every single place where people were working, forests were disappearing,' she recalled. 'It was an absolute shock.'

As she spoke out more and more about animals, Jane attracted many labels but she was never quite sure how she herself would name what she did. Her attitude changed regularly. Many people described her as an animal rights activist, but she denied this and said she didn't know what to call herself.[4] Jane saw many people campaign for animal rights but she felt that their goals could be of only limited use in isolation. Instead, she said, she was interested in 'human responsibility'.

She pointed out that across the world human rights are often ignored, even in places where people have signed bills recognizing these rights. So, she questioned just how effective these rights actually were. She argued that it was actually respect that truly mattered – for both humans and animals. She went on to explain that while human rights are important and may help in a court of law, they are not very helpful in situations such as bush meat hunting, where the hunters are unlikely to be influenced by such legislations.

Jane believed that sometimes the issue was about more than just the suffering of animals. Humans needed to take responsibility for their role in impacting the environment. While cruelty to animals was a pressing issue, the agricultural impact on the land was also a significant factor. Jane argued that agro-industry is one of the major contributors to climate change and biodiversity loss, with 'vast areas of land' cleared.[5] Something needed to change and she was going to use her platform to make a difference.

Did You Know?

On Valentine's Day 2023, Jane wrote that 'the natural world is desperately hoping for a Valentine's Day gift from each one of us . . . A traditional gift to a loved one is flowers. But let our gift to nature be to protect her flowers that they may provide nectar for bees and other pollinators.'[6]

A Rising Star

Recognition for Jane's work was building along with her fame. There is one story where Jane got in a taxi in London to go to Heathrow airport and the driver recognized her as an advocate for animals. He told Jane that his sister was working in conservation but he didn't see the need for it. Despite their differing views, they went on to have a long conversation where Jane told the driver about her work with chimpanzees and her amazing stories from Gombe. By the end of the trip he wasn't convinced, but she later received a letter from his sister to say that her brother had been to help her with her work![7] She often remembered this story to show the power of conversation.

Her advocacy for animals knew no boundaries. One time, she visited the home of the pop star Michael Jackson, and told him off for keeping his pet chimp Bubbles. 'I knew absolutely that what he was doing was wrong. And I was more than happy to tell him so. I said, "You know I don't approve of putting clothes on chimps, because it's disrespectful." I think he understood. But, you know, he was run as a sort of show, really, by his people. A lot of the things he did were things that he was told to do.'[8]

Jane also owned a pet monkey – but not a real one. During the 1990s, she was given a stuffed toy for her birthday, which she named Mr H. Mr H 'swung through more than sixty countries', according to the Canadian branch of the Jane Goodall Institute. In 1999, she estimated that Mr H had been 'touched, patted or kissed by well over two hundred thousand people'.

'He was given to me . . . by a man called Gary Haun, who became a magician and taught himself to paint after he was blinded at the age of 21', she explained. 'The monkey represents the indomitable human spirit overcoming obstacles and has accompanied me to sixty-one of the sixty-three countries I've visited.'

Some public attention was less welcome, however. In 1987, the US cartoonist Gary Larson drew a typically surreal *Far Side* sketch of two apes sitting on a branch. The female picks something out of the male's fur and asks in the manner of a suspicious wife, 'Well, well, another blonde hair . . . Conducting a little more "research" with that Jane Goodall tramp?'

The executive director of the Jane Goodall Institute was furious. He consulted a lawyer and sent fuming letters to the newspapers that ran the cartoon. However, when Goodall found out about it she was amused. 'Wow! Fantastic!' she said. 'Real fame at last!'

She offered to pen an introduction to Larson's forthcoming anthology, and he gave her Institute permission to put the cartoon on a fundraising T-shirt. But when Larson later visited Goodall's research centre in Tanzania, a chimp named Frodo grabbed him and pulled at his arm.[9] Perhaps a lesson learned.

Did You Know?

Jane ate some exotic and unfamiliar foods during her travels, but there was one she loved best. She was in the middle of nowhere in a forest in the northern Republic of Congo one evening, when they picked orange mushrooms, along with a large leaf from a low-lying plant. When they cooked them, the leaves made a kind of broth. 'It was absolutely delicious, and the vibrant orange and green colours were so beautiful,' she recalled.[10]

Caring for the Next Generation

Jane was passionate about education. In 1991 she founded Roots & Shoots, a non-profit organization which brought together young people from preschool to university age to work on environmental, conservation and humanitarian projects. The name was symbolic from the start.

'Roots creep underground everywhere and make a firm foundation,' she explained. 'Shoots seem very weak, but to reach the light, they can break open brick walls. Imagine that the brick walls are all the problems we have inflicted on our planet. Hundreds of thousands of roots and shoots, hundreds of thousands of young people around the world, can break through these walls. You can change the world.'[11]

Jane understood that children's formative years were deeply important for shaping how they would see the world. 'Give me a child up until age seven, and I'll have him for life,' she said. 'It's really true that people do get so much of who they are from those early years.'[12]

When Jane spoke to young people, she kept her message simple and inspiring. 'You can't solve the world's problems, so don't try,' she would tell them. 'Instead, focus on what you can do each day to leave this place a little better than you found it.'[13]

When she was interviewed by National Geographic Kids, she was asked to advise young people who wanted to have a 'wild career' like hers. 'You've got to really, really want it!' she said. 'You could go to university and go straight into research, but there are also lots of opportunities for volunteering or for working at one of the good zoos. Join Roots & Shoots while you're at school and don't give up! Keep your ears open for opportunities.'[14]

Jane's last message for Roots & Shoots was a reminder about peace. She said that peace is not simply the absence of war, but also the presence of respect, compassion and harmony with the natural world. She highlighted the many challenges: conflict and displacement, violence in communities, the climate crisis, and the destruction of our environment but Jane always ended with a message of hope. 'Through Roots & Shoots, young people in more than 75 countries are showing that every individual matters, every

action counts, and together we can create change. From protecting wildlife to supporting people in need and restoring the environment, their projects are proof that small, positive actions can add up to something powerful.'[15]

> Did You Know?
>
> One of Jane's more curious dreams was that she has always wanted yetis to be real. 'Now you'll be amazed when I tell you that I'm sure that they exist,' she told a podcast. 'I've talked to so many Native Americans who have all described the same sounds, two of whom have seen them. Well, I'm a romantic so I always wanted them to exist.'

Jane On Tour

When Jane toured the world, speaking at events and to broadcasters to raise awareness for her work, she charmed audiences wherever she went. On one occasion she announced that the world would be 'infinitely better off without men'. The interviewer asked her whether she meant humankind or men specifically. 'No, both,' she said. 'Well, women have been overpopulating the world with a considerable help from the men of course.'[16]

On her lecture tours, Jane would happily sign books, but also programmes, tickets and brochures. One time, the queue was so long that people queued for more than four hours. 'For me this period of signing is important because it gives me a chance to make contact with those who were in the audience,' she said. During her talk, Jane often used up all her energy and was left feeling 'empty and cold'. But the people she met at the signings changed that. 'These people are feeding you, aren't they?' a colleague suggested. Jane agreed.

When the conservationist Rick Barongi first met Goodall, she was 'delightful – sharp, funny, and endlessly curious', he remembered. But, like the porter at Peter Jones, he said he 'could also feel Jane's eyes studying me, like she was quietly assessing my character and motivation'.[17] Rick remembered some interesting and fun conversations they had on the long flights they took together. Jane 'never slept much, usually preferring to stay up late talking and sipping her single malt Scotch whisky (no ice and just a pinch of water)', he said. She sometimes displayed childlike enthusiasm, like when 'she wanted to put on the silly pyjamas provided by Air France just to get a picture, but fell asleep before she had the opportunity'.[18]

Throughout her life, she was often told that she was surprisingly energetic. This was true, but it didn't mean she didn't get tired sometimes. If Jane had a penny for every time someone commented on her energy levels, she might have amassed a small fortune. One cameraman who was tasked to follow her around to make a film about her said, 'Jane, I saw you. You were in the green room getting ready for a lecture, you were absolutely exhausted.

You were saying, "Just tell the people out there I've had to go into emergency, that I'm sick, I can't give a lecture." But something happened and you totally changed and you gave the best lecture I've ever heard you give.'[19]

She continued to find her lecture tours exhausting but said they left her mentally and spiritually enriched as she was able to explore different cultures, cities and people. Quite a turn-around for someone who was so painfully shy as a child.

That childhood shyness had never left her, but she had developed ways to deal with it. At the beginning when she'd received a letter from Louis Leakey telling her that *National Geographic* wanted her to do a series of lectures, she wasn't particularly thrilled by the news. 'I prayed to break a leg or something so that I wouldn't have to do it.' But she soon gained confidence as she found she could do it. 'I found that words came, I found that I could make people laugh. And eventually, I found I could make people cry.'[20]

Despite all the challenges, Jane's determination ran deep to the core of her life's mission. 'Every single one of us matters, has a role to play, and makes a difference'.[21]

Did You Know?

Jane believed there were symbols of hope wherever she looked, from a little plant coming up through concrete, to a child who survived cancer.

By the late 1990s, Jane was travelling three hundred days a year to give lectures, media interviews and attend business meetings. She would carry with her a packed suitcase, which she nicknamed 'the coffin' because of how heavy it always was with all the books and papers she took on the road.

There were some aspects of travelling she was less than keen on. 'I cannot tell you how I loathe packing,' she said. 'Somehow everything you own has babies on the road: it gets bigger, it grows. I should be an expert by now but I'm always in too much of a rush to pack. Everything I want is at the bottom, so everything erupts out.'[22]

She would carry some outfits with her: a couple of simple dresses, some skirt-and-blouse combos, some turtleneck jumpers, some moccasin shoes, some more formal shoes and a number of belts. For food, she took a single-cup electric heating element to warm up soup and other simple dishes, and emergency supplies of Marmite, chocolate and fruit. She was happy to improvise for her snacks, sometimes toasting bread using a hotel iron.

She didn't need to eat much and yet she still kept her famed energy flowing. This was the source of much wonder among those she encountered. Many observed how peaceful she was and asked what her secret was. Was it religion, meditation, good sleep? People also wondered what was going on inside her mind. Does she really believe what she says? What does she really think, deep down? What is her philosophy of life? What is the secret ingredient for her optimism, her hope?

They got many of the answers in her book *Reason for Hope: A Spiritual Journey.* When it was published in 1999, Jane was anxious about what reviewers would say. 'I was convinced,' she told her biographer, Dale Peterson, 'that people were going to say, "Well, why should she think she has something to say on this subject?"' Naturally, the reviews were glowing.

In an interview, she was asked for her four most important reasons for hope, the word she has used so much in conversations, interviews, speeches and book titles. The first reason, she said, was 'The passion, determination and energy of young people, once they know the problems and are empowered to take action.'

The second was the human brain, because although 'we know other animals are way, way more intelligent than science used to admit', no animal could invent telescopes or computers that allow people to talk via Zoom from all around the world. 'Finally we are beginning to use our brains to solve some of the problems we have created,' she explained.

The other two reasons she gave for hope were the resilience of nature and 'the indomitable spirit that forces people to tackle seemingly hopeless problems' and so often succeed. 'We all have that spirit – we must nurture it and set it to work to make our world a better place for people, animals and the environment.'[23]

Jane has also explained another reason for her tirelessly optimistic disposition. 'I don't know a single problem where there isn't a group of people struggling to put that problem right,' she said in a Q&A session. 'I think that's the greatest hope. There are more people awake and more people who are understanding that only when we link our clever, clever brain with the human heart – love and compassion – can we attain our true human potential.'[24]

Although Jane always preached a message of hope, she never did so at the price of honesty. This was particularly true when she spoke about the plight of women. 'Generally, I suppose if you just added up the number of abused women it would probably far outweigh the privileged women,' she said. She believed that many countries around the world had not progressed very far in treating women with dignity, and they were still treated as second-class citizens. 'And then in our own so-called civilized countries, the amount of domestic violence that is uncovered all the time is shocking.'[25]

As well as violence, Jane recognized the ever-present pressure on women to look a certain way. She was not keen on succumbing to that pressure, even though she acknowledged it. 'Well, it's an unfortunate thing that happens,' she said. 'I mean, yes, you can have millions of face lifts and all these different things that women have done to

their bodies – whatever they're called, bum tucks and boob enhancements. But personally, well, a) I haven't the money for that, and b) I haven't got the time for it. And c) I mean, there are more important things to me than how you look. I think the most important thing is to keep active, and to hope that your mind stays active.'[26]

★ ★ ★

Jane didn't believe that hope was just wishful thinking but rather something tangible. She told an audience at the 2024 Climate Forward event organized by *The New York Times* that they should imagine a 'long, dark tunnel with a little star at the end representing hope'.

She firmly believed that having a support network was one of the most important things about her work. Social support in times of trouble was absolutely vital, she thought. During a visit to China, she had heard a story that helped her form that view. It was about two men called Jia Haixia and Jia Wenqi. They'd been friends since they were boys, but by the time they were in their thirties, Haixia was blinded and Wenqi had lost both his arms.

Together, they found a way to overcome their challenges and find a new purpose in life. 'Both had often talked about how the land around their village had become increasingly degraded since they were young,' Jane explained. Wenqi wanted to plant trees, but this would present obvious challenges because they didn't have any money, Haixia was blind and Wenqi had no arms. So Wenqi said he would be Haixia's eyes and Haixia would be his arms.

'They couldn't afford to buy seeds or saplings, so they decided to clone from branches cut from nearby trees,' she said. 'Haixia did the cutting while Wenqi directed him to the right place, and they walked from place to place with Haixia holding on to one of Wenqi's empty sleeves.'

At first, it all went wrong: of the eight hundred cuttings they planted in the first year, only two survived. They realized the land was too dry, so they found a way to water it. Eventually, they successfully planted over ten thousand trees.

'And that,' explained Jane in *The Book of Hope*, 'was a wonderful example of how friendship can give hope to the hopeless. And a marvellous illustration of what can be accomplished by the indomitable human spirit.'

Jane was a keen supporter of refugees. On World Refugee Day in 2016, the plight of refugees seemed more serious than it had for some time. The conflict in Syria alone had displaced more than twelve million people while other conflicts, persecution and poverty around the world had driven ever larger numbers to leave their homes. These were 'people – men, women, and children – who have escaped from countries torn apart by the horrors of war and violence,' she wrote. 'Or left their homes and all that they know in their desperation to find a future that is not blighted by crippling poverty. Or wanting to be reunited with family members who have already left.'[27]

Did You Know?

Jane was once asked how many times she thought she'd been photographed during her life. 'I honestly wouldn't like to think about it,' she replied. 'I could wallpaper a mansion.'[28]

Jane's Storytelling

The longer Jane lived, the more the world became attuned to the spiritual message she carried and embodied. Particularly in the West, she saw a transformation from stubborn defensiveness to a more open attitude to spirituality and higher consciousness. She remained essentially spiritual about nature.

In *Reason for Hope*, she included a poem she had written about a healing visit she had paid to Gombe, when she became 'lost in awe at the beauty around [her]'. She called the poem *The Little Angels of Trees and Flowers*.

She also drew on classic writers to describe the sanctity of nature. 'Shakespeare says it beautifully when he talks of seeing "books in the running brooks, sermons in stones, and good in everything",' she said. She got the same feeling when she experienced the awe and wonder of a beautiful sunset or when she observed the stars at night.

However, not everyone was comfortable with this. 'When you talk about spirituality, many people are uneasy or absolutely put off,' she told Douglas Abrams, co-author of *The Book of Hope*. 'They think of a touchy-feely tree-hugging hippie sort of thing. Yet more and more people are now realizing that we have become increasingly materialistic and that we need to reconnect spiritually with the natural world.

'In a way, our disconnect with nature is very dangerous. We feel we can control nature – we forget that, in the end, nature controls us.'[29]

Jane had to choose carefully how she advocated to audiences. 'I believe that storytelling is the most successful way of helping people understand the true nature of animals,' she said. Jane was never opposed to stories of technological progress, but she was opposed to the tendency for these stories to make humanity feel even more superior to the beings we share the planet with. 'You know we've got to lose this arrogance. Just because we've got a brain that can design a rocket to go to Mars – that doesn't mean that we have any more right to be on this planet than an octopus,' she said.[30]

'Of course, if you already understand that animals, like us, have personalities, minds and emotions, you will be sickened by secretly filmed footage in a factory farm. This was a really good way to connect with people,' she explained. 'When they first watch film of a cow chasing after a football, mooing in excitement, then hitting it back with her nose so that her owner can throw it again, they are more likely to feel empathy for the cow in a crowded dairy farm having her calf dragged away a few hours after birth, mother and child desperately calling to each other.'[31] Jane's experience in the limelight gave her a sharp insight into the best way to tell stories and, as her influence increased, her message was more vital than ever.

Chapter Four

Elder Stateswoman

2000–2015

'So, yes, there is hope . . . It's in our hands. It's in your hands and my hands and those of our children. It's really up to us.'

—Jane Goodall in a 2001 TED Talk[1]

A National Treasure

As her years advanced, Jane came to be regarded as a national treasure. Fittingly, in January 2000, she appeared on BBC Radio 4's *Desert Island Discs*, where guests have to choose the things they would like to have with them if they were stranded on a desert island. Her favourite recording was Dylan Thomas's *Under Milk Wood* read by Richard Burton, her book of choice was *The Lord of the Rings* by JRR Tolkien, and her luxury item was a pencil and paper. Other recordings she chose included 'Walking in the Air' from *The Snowman*, 'Memory' from *Cats* and Antonín Dvořák's *Cello Concerto in B minor.*

Other songs and compositions she enjoyed listening to during her life included 'Heal the World' by Michael Jackson, 'Walk Lightly on This World' by Katie Melua, and classical scores such as Bach's *Toccata and Fugue in D minor*, Beethoven's 'Ode to Joy' from *Symphony No. 9 in D minor*, and Schubert's *Symphony No. 9 in C major.*

In early 2000, Jane spoke to a thousand-strong audience of religious delegates from a hundred different countries at the United Nations' Millennium Peace Summit of Religious and Spiritual Leaders. Only two of the speakers at the gathering spoke on behalf of animals: a Hindu leader and Jane. During one interview, she noted that Buddhists and many Indigenous peoples believe that humans are part of the animal kingdom and that animals are our brothers and sisters.

She was asked what the voice of the natural world would be, if it spoke to us directly. She replied: '*Could you please give us space and leave us alone to get along with our own lives and our own ways, because we actually know much better how to do it than when you start interfering?*' It was a concise summary of the message she was carrying around with her, as she served as a voice for those beings who had no voice of their own.

The importance of human connection with nature is an objective fact, not a sentimental belief, she insisted. 'They've proven that it psychologically benefits us,' she said. 'And physically we benefit from connecting with nature. It just is.'[2]

Jane continued to feel exasperated by the foolishness of destroying the planet we live on and the short-term thinking that was behind this. She was baffled by the disconnect between cleverness of the human mind and the emotion of the heart. 'I think if we don't have a grounding in this humane part of us, we create a very dangerous animal indeed, the animal that can go out and make weapons of mass destruction and kill others far away by pressing a button, and destroying the environment to the detriment of the children of the future,' she said in a lecture.[3] 'We've just got this one Mother Earth,' she said frequently. It was considered bizarre to her that we are making short-term decisions rather than long-term goals when the very future of our species is at risk. And so she kept banging the drum for the planet and found ways to make her voice heard.

> Did You Know?
>
> Jane believed that the vast scale of the challenge she faced in her advocacy for animals and the climate helped to keep her young. Asked what the secret of her youthfulness was, she replied, 'There's so much to do'.

Tragedy struck when Jane's mother died in April 2000 at the age of ninety-four. 'To the very end her mind was sharp and clear, though her body was giving up a little more each day,' noted Jane in a Roots & Shoots newsletter. She said Vanne had 'joined the cloud contingent', and paid tribute to her, declaring, 'No one can ever have had a better, more supportive mother.'

When she was once asked what love smelled like, she replied 'burnt toast', which took her back to 'memories of my absolutely amazing, wonderful, and supportive mother'. She added, 'You know, she wasn't much of a cook, because she always

burned the toast. So that's such a nice smell – we always think of mum.'[4]

Asked what advice she would give to her younger self before she embarked on her remarkable journey, she harked back instead to the advice her mother had given her: 'I would not give her any advice other than what my mother had always taught me,' she said. 'It was she who brought me up to know the importance of listening to the views of others, but having the courage of your convictions if, at the end, you still feel you are right. To respect others and be honest.'[5]

When it's Hard to Hope

Jane continued to travel throughout her life, and continued to have mixed feelings about it. Speaking to *Time* magazine, she explained how mercurial her attitude to travelling was. 'When I do get back to England for three weeks solid or I'm doing my writing, the thought of packing up and setting off is literally scary,' she said. 'But when you're actually on the road, it's just a way of life, like a gypsy, I suppose.' Although Jane travelled frequently, she rarely had an actual holiday.

'Isn't it weird?' she said, of her jetting lifestyle. 'It happened gradually. If I'd been given a choice in the early days, I would not have chosen this, because I've lost my personal life. It's virtually gone. I'm just a commodity in a way.'[6]

It wasn't just her travel that flummoxed her. She barely recognized herself at all as she stepped on and off so many boats, planes and trains. 'It never ceases to amaze me that there's this person who travels around and does all these things,' she said. 'And it's me. It doesn't seem like me at all.'[7]

But Jane used her platform to influence change. In April 2001, she co-signed an open letter to the US president George W Bush, which was sent to *Time* magazine. The other signatories included former US president Jimmy Carter, former Russian leader Mikhail Gorbachev, George Soros and Stephen

Hawking, who signed with a fingerprint. 'We urge you to develop a plan to reduce US production of greenhouse gases,' they wrote. 'The future of our children – and their children – depends on the resolve that you and other world leaders show.' But a few months later the world was rocked by catastrophe.

On the morning of 11 September 2001, Jane woke up in New York. She was staying in her favourite hotel, the Roger Smith at 501 Lexington Avenue. She rose early and began to prepare for the day she had planned. Very soon, the footage of the terror attacks on the city changed her plans and those of much of the world's population. She thought it must be a hoax at first, and then realized it was only too real.

Writing in *Reason for Hope*, Jane remembered how there was 'an eerie silence, punctuated only by the clanging bells of the ambulances and the police-car sirens' and how out on the streets around her hotel there were small groups of people desperately trying to find out more. She said it felt as if everyone in the city was worrying about the fate of a loved one.

Seven days later, when the airports opened again, she flew to Portland, Oregon, to continue with her tour, promoting her latest children's book. As she sat on the plane, she felt anxious. Not because of the danger of a hijacking, but because she was about to speak to eight hundred high school students on the theme of 'A Reason for Hope.' In the immediate aftermath of the September 11 attacks, it was harder for her to see what reasons for hope there were.

'I felt the fear,' she told a TED audience later, but 'nevertheless, there was so much human courage, so much love and so much compassion'.[8]

This wasn't the first time she'd been close to terrorism. When she was due to give a speech at the Royal Overseas League in London, a large bomb was found at the venue, placed there ahead of a different conference on IRA terrorism. She had also been evacuated from airports and train stations because of bomb threats on five separate occasions.

In the immediate aftermath of the September 11 attacks, there was a lot of talk of the US military bombing Afghanistan and Iraq. The prospect of more violence appalled Jane.

As the US and UK moved ever closer to invading Iraq, she wrote to the-then United States Secretary of State Colin Powell on several occasions to express her disquiet. 'In such frightening times we must be Colin & Jane, not Goodall & Powell, doctor general,' she began, doing away with any formalities. 'I am praying for some kind of Divine intervention in the days ahead. I feel so fearful of the repercussions of an attack on Baghdad. Not only am I English, & UK & USA are lumped together, but my face is the wrong colour. In so many of the places where I spend my time around the world, I fear the anger against our two countries will erupt.'[9]

A deadline was set for the Iraqi president, Saddam Hussein, to surrender to the West's demands. On the eve of the deadline, Jane was staying in a cabin near the Platte River in Nebraska. She recalled how thousands of sandhill cranes descended outside the cabin and began to dance. 'For nearly two hours, first one group, and then another, danced, leaping up again and again with outstretched wings, picking up bits of straw and clods of earth and throwing them into the air,' she revealed in a Roots & Shoots newsletter. They were, she believed, 'sent to tell us that, however dark these days may seem, there will be peace at the end.'

Soon after that, at an event, a woman came up to Jane and handed her a small bell. 'If you're talking about hope and peace, ring this. This bell is made from metal from a defused landmine, from the killing fields of Pol Pot, where people are now beginning to put their lives back together after the regime has crumbled.' The bell was a great inspiration to Jane to keep going.

Did You Know?

Jane often opened her public talks, lectures and interviews with an imitation of a chimpanzee greeting call. 'That's good morning in chimpanzee,' she would explain.

Jane's Accolades

In 2002, the-then Secretary General Kofi Annan bestowed upon Jane the highest honour of the United Nations for her work towards creating a more peaceful world through Roots & Shoots. She became a UN Messenger of Peace.

However, Jane also won many, many other awards, including:

1970 Stott Science Award, Cambridge University, UK

1974 Gold Medal for Conservation, San Diego Zoological Society, USA

1974 Bradford Washburn Award from the Museum of Science in Boston

1980 Order of the Golden Ark, World Wildlife Award for Conservation

1984 J Paul Getty Wildlife Conservation Prize

1985 Living Legacy Award from the Women's International Center, USA

1987 The Albert Schweitzer Award of the Animal Welfare Institute, USA

1987 National Alliance for Animals Award

1988 Centennial Award, National Geographic Society, USA

1989 Anthropologist of the Year Award

1990 The Kyoto Prize in Basic Science from the Inamori Foundation, Japan

1991 The Edinburgh Medal, UK

1994 Diamond Jubilee Medal from Chester Zoo, UK

1995 The National Geographic Society Hubbard Medal for Distinction in Exploration, Discovery, and Research, USA

1996 Silver Medal from The Zoological Society of London, UK

1997 Royal Geographical Society / Discovery Channel Europe Award for A Lifetime of Discovery

1999 International Peace Award, Community of Christ, USA

2001 Master Peace Award

2001 Gandhi/King Award for Non-Violence, USA

2002 The Huxley Memorial Medal from the Royal Anthropological Institute of Great Britain and Ireland

2003 Commonwealth Club Centennial Medallion Award

2004 Dame of the British Empire, presented by HRH Prince Charles, UK

2005 Two Wings Award, Vienna, Austria

2006 French Légion d'Honneur

2008 Women of the Year Award for Environmentalist, *Glamour* magazine, USA

2010 Our Earth category of the Bambi, Germany

2014 Animal Defence and Anti-Vivisection Society, Person of the Year Award, British Columbia, Canada

2017 Special Award presented to Dr. Jane Goodall in recognition of your outstanding work in the conservation of Chimpanzees in Tanzania – Ministry of Natural Resources and Tourism, Tanzania National Parks

2021 The Templeton Prize from The John Templeton Foundation, UK

2022 The Stephen Hawking Medal for Science Communication

2025 The Presidential Medal of Freedom, USA

Jane was also awarded more than fifty honorary doctorates, including:

1988 University of North Carolina, Greensboro, N.C., USA

1997 University of Edinburgh Veterinary School, Edinburgh, Scotland, UK

2005 Syracuse University, USA

2005 Rutgers University, USA

2006 Open University of Tanzania

2007 Kyoto University, Kyoto, Japan

2008 University of Toronto, USA

2011 The American University in Paris, France

2018 Simon Fraser University, Canada

2020 Hasselt University, Belgium

Stories of Hope

As we've already seen, Jane believed that a good way to change the world is by telling stories. And this was even more crucial after the September 11 attacks. Stories were how it all began, according to Jane. 'Sitting around a campfire, in a cave, telling stories about what happened during the day.' And so stories about her travels and the people she met was how Jane communicated the urgency of her message. 'Arguing and pointing fingers doesn't get you anywhere, because the more you do that, the more the person is not really listening', she said.[10]

Instead, she told stories of how she had stood in Greenland with Inuit elders who told her that even in summer, the ice never used to melt here, as they watched icebergs crashing into the ocean. Or stories of people who had had to leave their island homes because of the rising sea levels, or the terrible damage inflicted by hurricanes, typhoons and flooding.[11]

While she wasn't afraid to share the haunting stories of decline, Jane also loved stories of redemption which showed the resilience of nature. She delighted in the knowledge that although humans have 'bashed' the planet 'for years', it could bounce back.

One such story she told in her book *Hope for Animals and Their World* involved the plight of the American whooping crane – an endangered species in the US.

'It's a wonderful story,' she said in an interview. The only known flock would fly from Texas to Canada each year but each year when they returned, there were fewer and fewer until there were no more than twenty-seven birds left. However, efforts were made to find their breeding place and a captive breeding programme was soon developed to boost numbers.

An ultralight aircraft was used to teach the endangered captive-bred whooping cranes a new one-thousand-two-hundred-mile migration route from Wisconsin to Florida. When Jane went to visit the project, she got to go up in an ultralight. 'It was one of the most amazing experiences,' she said. 'It's like being a bird because you're out there in the air and looking down at these beautiful birds. These are the adolescents, still with some golden, cinnamon feathers, and it's been very successful.'[12]

She also told the story of the American burying beetle, a species that may not have much cute appeal, but still plays a crucial role in its ecosystem. Jane felt the beetle was vital because it

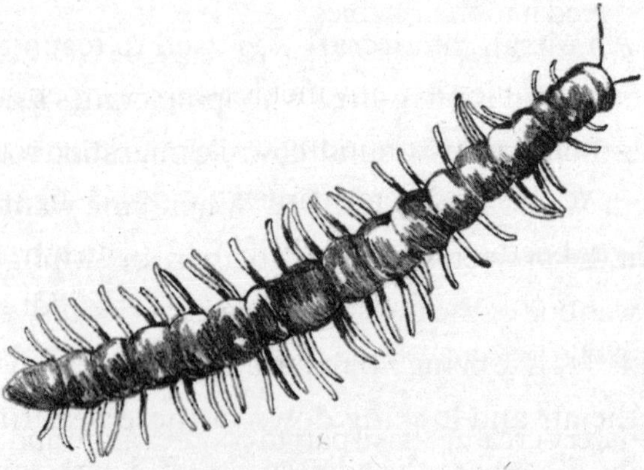

buries carrion, the remains of dead animals. She explained how if a small bird dies, the beetle will then bury it. A male beetle will then team up with a female and they will then bury the carcass together before mating. When the female lays her eggs on the carcass, they then also consume the carcass and feed it to their babies.

She recalled a funny incident that happened to one man who was working on the burying beetle project. 'He said a lady came along, and she said, "Your beetles look after their young much better than my children looked after my grandchildren." And the lady gave him $75,000.'[13]

Every creature has a part to play in nature and the environment, however objectionable that creature may be to human eyes. Jane used centipedes at Gombe to illustrate this point. 'They can grow to something like nine inches or a foot. They're very flat. They have a very poisonous bite. If you're allergic, they could kill you. They could probably kill a child. I once had one crawl up my leg. Fortunately, it climbed down. I just don't like them. But these centipedes are very good at making compost. They have a job to do, and they do it very well.'[14]

Jane was convinced that the care and help that we give back to the planet will have an impact. Nature will reclaim areas we've completely destroyed so that biodiversity, that glorious living web of life, can return. Animals on the brink of extinction can be given another chance.

Speaking in 2010, Jane explained once more how nature and the climate are connected to us all. 'And things which go on in let's say the Congo Basin, it may seem incredibly unimportant in the Midwestern United States, but then when you realize that the loss of the tropical forests in the Congo Basin is having an enormous effect on climate change, and climate change in turn is affecting weather patterns all over the world, then you start to realize that life is interconnected.' Everything is connected in nature and everything plays its part in the ecosystem.

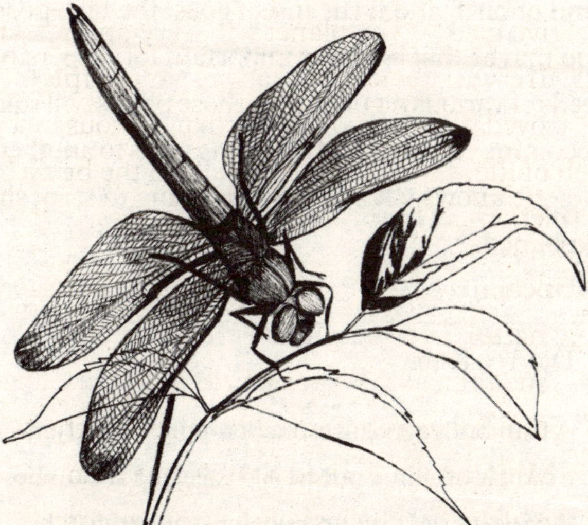

'There may be some small ecosystem and there may be an endangered species, it may be an insect and so what if it disappears, you know? But maybe that insect is the main prey of a certain kind of bird, and if the insect goes, the bird goes, and maybe that bird was important for dispersing seeds of various plants and so those plants will start becoming extinct – and one thing leads to another.' No one knows where all that is going to stop, she explained.[15]

Did You Know?

A Cambridge zoologist once proudly showed Jane a sample of chimp poo he had collected at Gombe during a brief visit years before she arrived, but Jane noticed right away that the stool was from a bush pig. 'I didn't tell him,' she confessed to *The New York Times*. 'What was the point?'

Looking Ahead

There is a well-known saying that goes, 'We have not inherited the world from our ancestors, we've borrowed it from our children'. But Jane strengthened the last part of the quote to 'we've stolen it from our children'. She explained why she made this change. 'If we cut down a forest that we are relying on for clean air and clean water, that's stealing the future, it's not borrowing. Because when you borrow, you pay back. How are we going to pay back a destroyed forest or a polluted ocean?'

New faces have started to emerge on the scene, taking the baton from Jane. In the summer of 2018, fifteen-year-old Greta Thunberg held the first School Strike for Climate outside the Swedish parliament. The protest quickly gathered momentum and saw Thunberg become a globally recognized climate activist. Thunberg has been arrested several times and her protests have attracted criticism as well as widespread admiration. Her confrontational style is in marked contrast to climate campaigners of yesteryear, such as Al Gore who made use of documentaries, Wangari Maathai who encouraged rural women to plant trees, and Jonathon Porritt who campaigned through political parties.

Naturally, Jane was often asked what she thought of this fascinating but polarizing Greta Thunberg. She viewed the rise of Thunberg and her youth movement with qualified admiration. Was it a good thing? 'Yes', she said, so long as people rolled up their sleeves and did something. More than just complaining to governments, Jane wanted to see young people taking action by planting trees and litter picking – only then could you approach the government to ask why they weren't doing more.

Jane also said that Greta had 'raised a lot of awareness, but for me demonstrating is not enough. And when you get very aggressive when you're talking to big business or governments, it turns many people off. But we're at the stage now where we need all approaches, so I think hers is doing a lot of good, and ours, which is the opposite, is too.'[16]

There are so many simple but helpful things people can do, Jane pointed out. 'My job seems to have increasingly become giving people hope, so that instead of doing nothing and sinking into depression, they take action'.[17]

When Jane was asked what people can do to help the planet, she would tell them to do simple things. 'Perhaps you can walk or cycle or take a train or bus instead of using a car. You can think about what you buy – when it was produced, did it harm the environment? Was it cruel to animals? Is it cheap because of unfair wages? Then search for a more ethically produced product. Will it cost more? Probably, but then you will value it more and waste less. And waste is a huge problem today.'[18]

One of the core messages of Jane's life was that every time we spend money, we can either become part of the problem or part of the solution. What you choose to buy can make a big impact, especially if you ask questions of it, she felt. 'If we all start to make ethical decisions about what we buy and eat and wear, this will cumulatively lead to a better world. Before this can happen we must alleviate poverty, because very poor people cannot afford to make those choices; they have to do what they must to survive.'[19]

Jane also encouraged her followers to 'think and pray and then follow where your heart leads you'.[20]

Jane was delighted when her grandchildren took up similar causes. Her son Grub and his wife Maria had three children – daughter Angel van Lawick and sons Merlin and Nick van Lawick. All three were raised in Tanzania and Angel and Merlin followed in their grandmother's footsteps.

In 2013, Angel began visiting the Jane Goodall Institute's Roots & Shoots clubs worldwide, and in May 2014, she spent a week volunteering for the Sonoma County Wildlife Rescue in California. Merlin, meanwhile, is a conservationist working with the Jane Goodall Institute, and a board member of the Earth Species Project.

But their father didn't really inherit this bug. 'He's never wanted to really go out there and study animals like that, so it didn't really appeal to him, but he does look back and remember the freedom of it and how beautiful it was,' Jane told Getty in November 2017.

Did You Know?

Jane didn't like being called 'darling', as an attendant on a flight once discovered after she used that name for her passenger. 'I was so mad at her, as if I was an old lady in a home,' Jane told *The Times*. 'I wanted to say to her, "I'm not your darling!" But I thought if I did she'd stop serving me.'

In 2015, Jane lost a man who had been so important to her life – her mentor Robert Hinde. Writing on her website, she praised him as part of 'the era of the first great early ethologists'. They met when she arrived at Cambridge, a meeting she felt 'understandably nervous' about.

'Poor Robert!' she recalled. She remembered how she would write enthusiastically about 'various aspects of chimp behaviour, struggling to fit my observations into something like the format expected of a "proper" scientist,' and would visit him at his rooms in St John's College, 'feeling not a little proud' of her work.

'As he discussed my efforts, I felt more and more horrified – all my carefully typed pages were liberally covered with criticisms, in red ink. Carefully he explained where I was not thinking like a scientist. I would get back to my digs and hurl the pages into a corner of the room, angry and hurt and, yes, defiant.

'But in the morning, after sleeping on it, I would pick up the pages. Read his comments carefully, and realize his reasons for the defilement of my work.' It seems that the humility Jane displayed in her attitude towards animals was also present in how she dealt with feedback on her work.[21]

Robert had a significant impact on Jane's career and she attributes the success of Gombe's research to him. It were these people in Jane's life that gave her the motivation to keep going with her mission of changing the world for the better. And she continued her advocacy right up to her later years.

Chapter Five

Later Years

2016–2024

'There is a growing awareness of the problems and also of the incredible progress that is being made in all sorts of technologies that can work against climate change.'

—Jane Goodall in an interview with *The Washington Post*[1]

Connecting With Others

Jane wielded considerable influence in the later years of her life as she met with politicians and influential people. Speaking of her lobbying technique, she said she was not aggressive. Even if she only had a few minutes in the hallway with a politician, she tried to be personal, finding a shared concern or inquiring about the health of a relative. 'You try and find something,' she told *The New York Times*. 'You would never just walk in and start talking.'

And yet, for someone with such a serious message, Jane also knew how to make people laugh. 'I think having a sense of humour is really important,' she said. 'At the start of a serious meeting, or during a talk, I ask the most important man to join me, and demonstrate to everyone how a female chimpanzee greets a dominant male, while telling him what he must do – look big and intimidating while I approach submissively, take his hand so that he pats my head and then, emboldened, embrace him and make pant grunts in his neck.' Sometimes, she would follow this up by asking everyone present to stand and greet their neighbours in the same way. 'This reduces tensions in the most important meetings!' she explained.[2]

When Jane met journalist Richard Godwin, within sixty seconds she started to nuzzle into him, to show how they would greet one another if they were chimpanzees. 'I'm the female, you're the big male and I'm a little bit nervous of you,' she told him. 'So, I come up with a submissive *akh akh akh!* . . . And you're completely quiet but you gently pat my head. That reassures me.'[3]

Jane's powers of persuasion were authentic: 'So when I meet somebody that I want to convince, I try to find something out about them that makes a link. Maybe they love dogs. Or something else. And then, listen. Because you might get a new idea, you may understand why they think the way they do. And that can be helpful in trying to change a mindset.'[4]

She explained the difference between intellect and intelligence during an interview with *The Washington Post*, hoping the distinction would encourage people not to destroy the ecosystem which was so vital to us. 'The intellect solves problems and it can do intricate mathematics and work out what's out there in the universe, galaxies and solar systems and so on,' she said. 'But if you are intelligent, you don't destroy your only home, that isn't intelligent. We seem to have lost wisdom.' So she continued to try to reach people's hearts as much as their minds. 'If one wants to reach people, if one wants to change attitudes, you have to reach the heart,' she said.

But she knew her limits and was aware that she couldn't change everyone. Some people were beyond help, she explained. 'Well, honestly, I hate to say it, but there's some people I don't think I could change. I think they're beyond it. I would say you couldn't have changed Hitler and you couldn't change Stalin, and there are people today I put in that category. So that's why I'm concentrating so much on young people, especially at university when they're about to come out into the big wide world.'[5]

One of many lives that Jane touched and transformed was that of twenty-three-year-old former NFL cheerleader Mireya Mayor. Although Mayor had no scientific background at that time, when she saw Jane's work, she wanted to follow in her footsteps.

'In large part because of her, I became a primatologist, co-discovered a new species of lemur in Madagascar and have had an amazing life and career, in science and on TV, as a National Geographic explorer,' wrote Mireya Mayor.

In 2011, Mayor published her memoir *Pink Boots and a Machete: My Journey from NFL Cheerleader to National Geographic Explorer*. Jane wrote in the introduction, 'Mireya Mayor reminds me a little of myself. Like me she loved being with animals when she was a child. And like me she followed her dream until it became a reality.'[6]

So Jane continued to have a positive impact around the world, and this was her mark of real success. On a visit to Burundi, she discussed with the French ambassador, Gerrit van Rossum, a problem with Burundi's Vyanda Forest Reserve. On her next visit, he told her that he'd persuaded France's government to come up with the cash to hire park rangers and address the issue.

'Can you imagine what it's like for me to hear, "Because of your last visit, we're doing this work"?' she asked a *New York Times* interviewer. 'You never know who it's going to be, or what they're going to do. But as long as I do it, it keeps happening. So you can see why I can't very well stop.'

Jane has an effect on businesses too. 'I was talking to the head of a big corporation in

Singapore,' she remembered. 'He said, "You know, Jane, our company is totally changing and for three reasons. One, we see the writing on the wall. We see that we cannot go on exploiting the finite natural resources of the planet. They're not infinite. They're being used up. Secondly, there's consumer pressure. As people get more educated and more passionate, they're not buying things if we make them unethically, if we don't attend to our supply chain." But he said the real thing came when his daughter came home from school and said, "Daddy, is what you're doing hurting the environment? Because I'm going to have to live in it, aren't I, when I grow up?" And he said, "That hurt me."'[7]

If it wasn't politicians or businesses Jane was speaking to, she was always trying to encourage conversations. The September 2019 issue of British *Vogue* was guest edited by the Duchess of Sussex, and for that special issue, the Duke of Sussex interviewed Jane Goodall about the state

of conservation. She told him that climate change was terrifying, particularly for Meghan and Harry, who had just had a baby. Harry laughed and said, 'I know!'

⋆ ⋆ ⋆

Speaking out on behalf of nature can begin to wear people down when they realize they are not changing the hearts and minds of everyone they speak to, even when they reveal the harsh truths and speak from the heart. Sometimes it can feel like speaking to a brick wall. How did Jane keep going when there were people that had such strong views against her own? How did she persevere when people seemed to show indifference to her message? Despite the setbacks Jane remained resolute to keep pushing for change.

She reasoned, 'on the other side of the coin, there is a growing awareness of the problems and also of the incredible progress that is being made in all sorts of technologies that can work against climate change.'[8]

All this reaching out was hard work and the more respected Jane became, the more demands she had on her time, which inevitably took its toll. When a Tanzanian border guard shone the light of his mobile onto Goodall's face to match it with the photo on her passport, he remarked that she looked tired. 'You'd be tired, too,' she responded. 'I've given lots of speeches today, to ministers and ambassadors.'

Did You Know?

Jane's favourite colour was green, but she said there were times she liked blue as well.[9]

Dreams of Gombe

Jane's extensive travel later in life meant there were a lot of places to choose from when asked about those she loved. In an interview with *Wanderlust* magazine, she shared, 'I think my favourite places mostly relate to the people. I love

Taiwan: we have six hundred and fifty Roots & Shoots groups across the island, and we're linking up school gardens to make a corridor for indigenous butterflies.' She added, 'I love parts of the US – Yellowstone, for example, and the migration of the sandhill cranes and snow geese in Nebraska. They come to the Platte River on their way north every March; millions come in each night, millions. It really is one of the seven wonders of the world.' [10]

In 2017, National Geographic released a documentary with lots of archive footage of Jane's family, a warm reminder of her old home in Gombe. 'It's got Grub when he's a little gorgeous baby. I'd forgotten how beautiful he was,' she told Smithsonian. 'I loved seeing Grub when he was small – on the beach and swimming with the baboon and that sort of thing.' She wasn't sure how Grub would take to the documentary, which included footage of his birth. But he loved it, she told Fox News, though he said he 'didn't feel at all connected to that little baby'.

Jane's heart was always in the Gombe forests, she said, because the best days of her life were spent there. People sometimes asked her why she wasn't still there but it was no longer the same place she lived back in her younger years. When she returned to Gombe with *The New York Times*, there were a lot of tourists there. When a colleague asked her, 'Where do you want to go?', she replied, 'Away from all these people'. She was asked how different Tanzania was from her early years there. 'Well, everything's changed', she said. 'The Serengeti was just wild; there wasn't even a road to Olduvai. Now the wilderness around Gombe is basically gone – villages have sprung up – but it's still not one of the main tourist routes, thank goodness.'[11]

Another of Jane's favourite places on earth was her family home at Bournemouth on the south coast of England. She could 'look out of my window at the trees that I climbed when I dreamed of Tarzan and going to Africa,' and there she could remember Gombe as it was when she was young. This was the home she described for *The Times* newspaper in 2022, which she'd called home since the 1930s. 'It has two storeys and an attic, which I converted into my haven, where I work. It's quite simple – I don't have a style; I don't really care,' she said. 'There are books everywhere, in every single room, and in the long passages to the loos – we don't have en suites. Books from my grandmother, huge illustrated Bibles from her clergyman husband, my childhood books (lots of Tarzan), my sister's music books, my uncle's medical books, books on natural history, masses of poetry.'

Despite her busy schedule, in the middle of the day Jane would take a thirty-minute break 'to sit under the beech tree in the garden, as I used to do as a child. I'll have a bit of toast, cheese and tomato. And every day I'm joined by a blackbird and a robin and I sing nonsense to them.'

She said the house always smelled of dog, and roses in the summer because 'we always have them'.[12] Dogs had been a constant presence throughout Jane's life but at that stage they had a very aged whippet, called Bean. Although the family rescued him, it was the first time the house had had a dog she couldn't bond with. 'He's aloof, more like a cat,' she said. 'Dogs have taught me so much . . . so faithful and give unconditional love, and I don't like to think of a world without dogs.'

The Quirks of Jane Goodall

But what of the lesser-known aspects of Jane's life? Wherever she was in the world, she kept up the spirit of a family tradition. 'I drink a whisky every night,' she told *The Guardian*. It was a ritual because she and her mum always used to have 'a small glass together at home'. She continued, 'As I travelled more, we'd each raise a glass at our respective 7pms. It was a way to feel connected.

Now I toast her up in the clouds every evening. Of course, it's for medicinal purposes.'[13]

Jane once said that, to her, success smelled like 'being around your friends when some exciting news has come through, waving a glass with a little touch of Scotch whisky in it'.[14]

During an interview with *The Times*, she explained that she had problems with her voice, and showed the interviewer a small bottle of whisky. 'It's the only thing, I tell you. I've talked to four opera singers and one pop singer and asked what they do when their voice gets tired and they all said whisky.'[15]

In order to piece together the Oscar-nominated documentary *Jane*, director Brett Morgen made use of more than a hundred hours of raw colour footage that had been taken at Gombe in the early years and filed away unseen in the National Geographic archives for over fifty years. Jane reluctantly agreed to give Morgen a three-hour interview for the documentary, but she ended up spending three days chatting to him. 'There are people who interview you and are so stupid,' she told the *Belfast Telegraph*. 'I mean they don't know what to ask and then I don't want to talk to them. Brett knew what he was talking about.' She said that every time Morgen saw her, he either cried or giggled. 'Everyone says that I have a very odd effect on him.' The result of their work and Brett's tears was a unique, intimate portrait of Jane, which was praised as remarkable by *Deadline*.[16]

Jane was honoured in a different way when Mattel made a Barbie doll of her. Part of the Barbie Inspiring Women series, paying tribute to 'incredible heroines of their time; brave women who took risks, changed the rules, and paved the way for generations of girls to dream more than ever'. The collectible doll was made from recycled materials and came accompanied by chimpanzee David Greybeard. Jane's doll wore

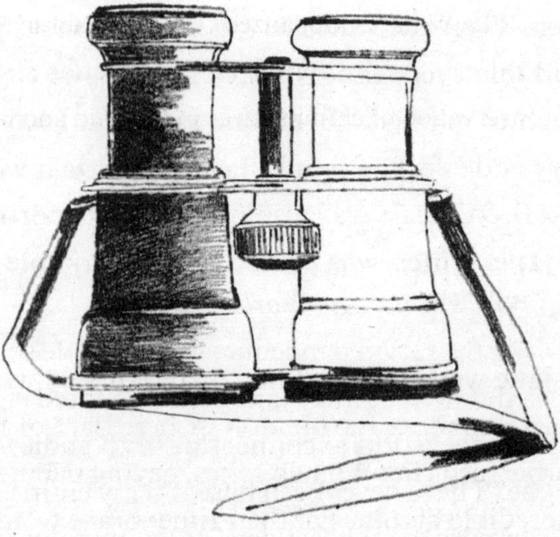

field clothes and came equipped with binoculars and a notebook.

> Did You Know?
>
> In 2018, World Chimpanzee Day was established to raise awareness for the care, protection and conservation of chimpanzees in the wild and in captivity.

When the World Changed

During the Covid pandemic, many people's lives slowed down, but not Jane's. She pivoted from touring the world to connecting with audiences online. 'I have never been busier in my entire life, except perhaps the last days of trying to get my PhD thesis written,' she said in an interview with *The Independent*. She felt it was important to focus on the positive things that emerged during the pandemic. 'And hundreds of people who live in big cities around the world have breathed clean air and seen the stars in a clear night sky, and heard the singing of birds loud and clear, no longer drowned by the roar of passing traffic. Marine life is experiencing the joy of a world no longer contaminated by the constant noise of shipping and man-made sonar technology.'

She also praised the many heroes who emerged, 'Doctors, nurses and other care givers on the front lines are at risk every day – and too often they are losing their lives as countries struggle to provide sufficient protective gear to keep them safe.'[17]

Jane pinpointed the problem at the heart of the pandemic. 'As we destroy the environment, animals are living in smaller and smaller spaces, and viruses are transferring from one animal to another,' she said. Wildlife trafficking, the handling of wild animals, meat markets and the bushmeat trade also added to the problem, she believed. 'This is where a virus gets the opportunity to jump from animals into people, and that's what happened with Covid-19.' Jane pointed out that a pandemic 'had been predicted' and even though people 'knew it was coming, they talked about it but nobody did anything'.[18]

One new project that kept her busy was when the Jane Goodall Institute introduced 'Virtual Jane', allowing her to successfully connect with audiences through remote lectures, recordings and her podcast, the *Jane Goodall Hopecast*. Among her guests were US senator Cory Booker, author Margaret Atwood and marine biologist Ayana Elizabeth Johnson.

During the pandemic at the end of 2021, Archbishop Desmond Tutu died. Jane paid fulsome tribute and recalled her horror when she first set foot in Cape Town as a young woman and saw the reality of apartheid. At the end of her tribute, she told the deceased Tutu, 'You will surely be rewarded and praised in the world that lies waiting for the spirit of the deserving after leaving their earthly bodies. But don't lose your sense of humour and impish chuckle.'[19]

On 8 September 2022, it was announced that Queen Elizabeth II had died. Jane said it was 'hard to imagine' a Britain without her. In 1979, Jane and Derek had attended a reception in Africa for the British royal family. They had what they described as an informal chat with the Queen, who told Jane she had watched a documentary about her work.

Did You Know?

When the Ziwa Rhino and Wildlife Ranch in Uganda named a rhino calf after Jane, she said she was honoured, adding, 'I am so looking forward to the day when I can meet her, face to face – or face to horn!'[20]

As Jane reached her nineties, her work continued. 'There's so much left to do. As long as my mind and body obey, I'll keep at it.' On the morning of her ninetieth birthday, she told a *New York Times* reporter that even on her big day her focus was to try to get the world to take action on climate change and biodiversity loss. 'That's why I'm traveling three hundred days a year,' she said. 'It's no good just talking about what should be done. We've got to flipping well do it.'

'There's no good sitting . . . and wishing that that hope would come to us,' she said. 'We've got to roll up our sleeves. The Bible says, gird your loins. I love that. I'm not quite sure what it means, but let's gird our loins. And we've got to climb over, crawl under, work around all the obstacles.'[21]

On the International Day of Peace in 2024, Jane gave a message of unity. 'Just imagine what the world would be like if everyone paid heed to the Golden Rule common to every single major religion: 'Do to others as you would like them to do to you,' and those 'others' should include animals and Mother Nature, she said.[22]

That year, she visited twenty-seven countries, including Australia, New Zealand, India, Malaysia, Nepal, Hong Kong, Slovakia and Colombia with her message of hope. One of her appearances was at a gathering of ninety dogs on a beach in California.

Speaking to the BBC about what kept her going, she was clear. 'Surely people want a future for their children,' she said. 'If they do, we have to get tougher about [environmental] legislation. We don't have much time left to start helping the environment. We've done so much to destroy it.'[23]

She simply refused to stop fighting for nature. 'I mean I have to go on, don't I? It's a gift. If you have a gift and you don't use it, it's not very good.'

Did You Know?

When an interviewer asked Jane when she would take a rest, she replied, 'What is that word?' She admitted that she worried about her 'carbon footprint with flying everywhere, but I don't have a magic carpet', she said.[24]

Chapter Six

A Legacy of Love

'I'll die fighting, that's for sure.'

—Jane Goodall in an interview with
The Guardian[1]

Final Days

In the final days of her life in the autumn of 2025, Jane was still busy. She was on stage in New York one day and discussing her work on a *Wall Street Journal* podcast two days later. She was due to appear at an event reflecting on her long life and career in Los Angeles on 3 October, before another event in Washington, DC the following week, but died of natural causes on 1 October 2025.

On the morning of 12 November, more than one thousand five hundred people gathered to celebrate her extraordinary life at her funeral service at the imposing neo-Gothic National Cathedral in Washington, DC. It was livestreamed for supporters, admirers and mourners around the world.

An urn containing Jane's ashes, draped in white cloth, was on show as bells tolled solemnly. A stuffed chimpanzee clutching a banana sat perched on a narrow wooden rail at the front of the pews.

The service included personal tributes from four speakers, readings from Jane's family and leaders from the Navajo and Cherokee nations, plus music from Grammy award-winning violinist Joshua Bell, National Symphony Orchestra youth members, Children of the Gospel Youth Choir, and the Washington National Cathedral musicians.

The ninety-minute service was officiated by Bishop Mariann Edgar Budde, who said, 'While Jane felt singularly and distinctly called to live fully the life God had given her, as you well know, part of her life's mission was to persuade all of us to live such lives ourselves.' She called Jane 'a human being fully alive'. Trying to sum up Jane's message, she declared, 'Get up. Go ahead. Do something. Move to preserve our beautiful planet for all living beings.'[2]

Guests at the memorial service were greeted upon arrival with a twenty-dog salute from People Animals Love therapy dog teams. As they left the cathedral, they were sent off by a giant peace

dove puppet, carried by young Roots & Shoots members. Additional tributes and memorial services took place around the world in the months following the funeral, further celebrating the life of the global conservation icon.

⋆ ⋆ ⋆

Many spoke about Jane in the days that followed. Francis Collins, the physician and geneticist who led the Human Genome Project, said that Jane 'appealed to our better angels'. Jane's conversations 'were always unfailingly gracious and informative,' he said.

Her eldest grandson, Merlin van Lawick, said that his grandmother 'constantly reminded us that life was full of wonders'. He promised to carry on her mission: to think with a 'clever human brain', to act with a 'compassionate human heart', to live by her maxim that every individual matters. 'The seeds of hope you have planted have taken root in millions,' he said affectionately. 'You will live on in countless hearts.'

The Executive Director of the Jane Goodall Institute USA, Anna Rathmann, said that 'Jane was never the loudest in the room. In fact, quite the opposite. But her powerful message spoke volumes'.

'Yes, she could be clear-eyed, even blunt about the greed and relentless consumption of our species,' said the actor and climate campaigner Leonardo DiCaprio. 'But beneath that fierce honesty was an unwavering faith that every voice matters, that we are all connected to the living world, and that each of us can make a difference.'[3]

Naturally, tributes poured in for some time after she died. Sir David Attenborough spoke of Jane in terms of her friendship with animals and the breakthroughs that this led to. 'Jane Goodall was the first to prove that an investigating scientist and a great ape living in the wild could become true friends, and in doing so, she came to transform our understanding of chimpanzees,' he said. 'She

was their tireless advocate and a great champion of environmental protection.'

The former US president Barack Obama, who met Jane when he was campaigning for the White House, chose to praise her inspirational nature. 'Jane Goodall had a remarkable ability to inspire us to connect with the natural wonders of our world, and her groundbreaking work on primates and the importance of conservation opened doors for generations of women in science,' he said.

António Guterres, Secretary-General of the United Nations, said Jane was 'leaving an extraordinary legacy for humanity and our planet'.

Harry and Meghan remembered how Jane held their son, Archie, when he was first born. She 'showered love and care to those who were privileged to know her,' they said. Prince William said Jane's 'boundless curiosity, compassion and pioneering spirit transformed our understanding of the natural world'.

Professor Ben Garrod, biologist at the University of East Anglia who worked closely with Jane, noted that she 'was often the quietest person in the loudest room, who would have the greatest impact'. The broadcaster Chris Packham said that she 'died on her job, trying to communicate the urgent need to confront climate breakdown and biodiversity loss'.

'Although it feels as though the colour has drained from the world a little with the passing of this great conservation elder,' said Dr Philippa Brakes from the Whale and Dolphin Conservation, 'Jane's boundless optimism and unshakable belief in humanity remind us what we can all do, individually and collectively'.

Ian Redmond OBE, Born Free's Policy Advisor and great ape expert, said that as well as her scientific and humanitarian legacy, he would 'equally remember her for the mischievous twinkle in her eye and her ability to hold an audience in the palm of her hand, inspiring every one of us lucky enough to be in the room to do better, in our daily lives, for our community, for animals and for the planet'.

Having started in one small research camp in Tanzania, Jane's work eventually inspired millions of people worldwide. There is no better example of the message that one person can make all the difference in the world.

The Legacy of Jane Goodall

In the closing years of her life, Jane became a true icon but she struggled to come to terms with this status. Jane remained baffled by it. She was rarely lost for words but when an interviewer asked what it was about her work that connects people to her, she wasn't sure what to say. 'I wish I could answer that question,' she said. 'I wish somebody could explain it to me.

'I mean, how did I become this icon? I don't know. I just feel like me. I guess I've had a lucky life. I guess I've learned the right lessons. I guess the right path has been laid before me, and I just have to make the right choices. But why people want to listen to me and take comfort very often, I don't know.'[4]

Often her way of dealing with the attention was to share it: she was always happy to shine the spotlight onto what other people were doing. 'Unfortunately, the media believes (maybe rightly) that bad news sells,' she said. 'So far more space is given to the bad news. But there are so many amazing people, so many incredible projects proving that you can turn things around.' Children, especially, are finding out that they can make a difference, she said.[5]

Jane's work showed her firsthand the impact of humanity on so much of nature and the ecosystem that supports us all. 'What's so fascinating is the more I've lived and travelled and talked with people and seen with my own eyes, the more I realize how interrelated everything is,' she said. 'There are stories where, you know, one little insect or plant or something becomes extinct, and

it doesn't seem to matter, but it turns out that that was a major food source for another creature. And so, gradually, there's a chain reaction, and you can have an entire ecosystem collapse just because one piece was taken out, and we didn't realize what that would do.'[6]

Jane's travel and experience gave her an insight that we would be wise to heed. 'Everywhere in our world there are problems,' she said. 'But everywhere there are problems, I find a group of caring, compassionate, dedicated, courageous people who are working for little or no money, who are risking their health, sometimes risking losing their lives, to try and put those problems right. And it's this which gives me the greatest hope. Perhaps, and I hope, at last, we're beginning to see the ice melting in the human heart.'[7]

Right until the end, Jane continued to change the hearts and minds of all sorts of people, but not least the young.

And so, Jane's ultimate legacy shows us that animals are friends we share the planet with, rather than strangers to be ignored, commodified or exploited. She showed us how their fate is ultimately our fate and that until all of us are protected and cared for, none of us are. She also showed us that we don't have to follow the normal path and that hope is a powerful tool.

When National Geographic asked Jane what she was most proud of, she said, 'Helping people to understand – thanks to the chimps – that humans are part of the animal kingdom, not separate from it. When I started out, nobody else was studying chimps in the wild, so I was able to show how their behaviour is like ours – kissing, cuddling, holding hands, patting one another, giving reassurance etc.'[8]

Perhaps the world is more connected than we like to think; and perhaps this demands our attention as much as it did the attention of the wise Jane Goodall. But we close with Jane's words, as

she looked back over her own life and speculated on what was to come next for her after her life ended.

Jane explained that she had felt personally guided by a higher intelligence. 'I don't know what to call this higher being, but I feel it very much in the forest, this deep spiritual connection,' she said. 'I love it that so many top scientific brains have also come to this conclusion that there is an intelligence behind the universe.'[9]

She said she had been told by 'very spiritual people' that she had an old soul, or a soul that had been through many incarnations. She expanded on her thoughts on reincarnation in an interview for *The Independent*. 'Living and dying – it's a cycle and we're in the cycle,' she said. 'Maybe we have to go through different phases to get to whatever the end is. I don't know. But that's going to be the next great adventure, finding out!'[10]

Acknowledgements

Thanks to Jessica Minocha for commissioning this book and for her kindness and wisdom. Thanks to Nicola Crane for commissioning me to write its predecessor: *The Wit & Wisdom of David Attenborough*. Thanks also to Louisa Johnson. With special thanks to Rimsha Falak and copyeditor Joanna Smith, and proofreader Chris Stone.

About the Author

Chas Newkey-Burden writes about animal rights, veganism and climate change for *The Guardian*, *The Spectator*, *The Independent*, *The I Paper*, *Metro*, *The Daily Telegraph* and *Byline Times*. He speaks at animal rights events and has run several marathons to raise funds for animal-free research and animal sanctuaries.

He is the author of dozens of books, including *The Wit & Wisdom of David Attenborough*, *Running: Cheaper Than Therapy*, *The Runner's Code*, *The Reduced History of Dogs* and *Taylor Swift: The Whole Story*. He is the host of *Jesus Christ, They've Done It: The Threads Podcast*.

Bibliography

In the Shadow of Man by Jane Goodall (1971), W&M

Jane Goodall: A Biography by Meg Greene (2005), Prometheus Books

Jane Goodall: The Woman Who Redefined Man by Dale Peterson (2006), Mariner Books

Reason for Hope: A Spiritual Journey by Jane Goodall and Phillip Berman (1999), Grand Central Publishing

The Book of Hope: A Survival Guide for Trying Times by Jane Goodall and Douglas Abrams (2021), Viking

Endnotes

Chapter One

1 *Reason for Hope: A Spiritual Journey* by Jane Goodall and Phillip Berman (1999), Grand Central Publishing

2 *Reason for Hope: A Spiritual Journey* by Jane Goodall and Phillip Berman (1999), Grand Central Publishing

3 *Jane Goodall: The Woman Who Redefined Man* by Dale Peterson (2006), Mariner Books

4 Ibid

5 https://learningenglish.voanews.com/a/what-it-takes-jane-goodall/4364308.html

6 *Jane Goodall: The Woman Who Redefined Man* by Dale Peterson (2006), Mariner Books

7 https://faceblind.livejournal.com/5325.html

8 https://www.nbcdfw.com/entertainment/the-scene/perot-museum-exhibition-illuminates-jane-goodalls-personal-journey-mission/3009894/

9 https://www.forbes.com/sites/marianneschnall/2025/10/03/the-life-and-legacy-of-dr-jane-goodall-her-timeless-words-of-wisdom/

10 https://news.lafayette.edu/2013/05/08/transcript-of-jane-goodalls-speech-and-qa-session/

11 https://news.janegoodall.org/2025/06/03/jane-goodall-farm-animals-are-sentient-and-often-sapient/

12 *Jane Goodall: The Woman Who Redefined Man* by Dale Peterson (2006), Mariner Books
13 https://www.dumbofeather.com/conversations/jane-goodall-is-a-primatologist/
14 *Reason for Hope: A Spiritual Journey* by Jane Goodall and Phillip Berman (1999), Grand Central Publishing
15 Ibid
16 https://a24films.com/notes/2025/04/ambassador-of-the-heart-with-isaiah-saxon-jane-goodall
17 https://awpc.cattcenter.iastate.edu/2025/10/02/un-messenger-of-peace-dr-jane-goodall-addresses-the-climate-assembly-aug-14-2023/
18 *The Book of Hope: A Survival Guide for Trying Times* by Jane Goodall and Douglas Abrams (2021), Viking
19 *Reason for Hope: A Spiritual Journey* by Jane Goodall and Phillip Berman (1999), Grand Central Publishing
20 https://news.mongabay.com/2013/08/coming-to-terms-with-the-evil-jane-goodall-and-the-mystery-of-the-dragonfly-incident/
21 https://www.theguardian.com/science/2023/feb/18/jane-goodall-people-are-surprised-i-have-a-wicked-sense-of-humour
22 https://news.janegoodall.org/2021/09/11/dr-jane-goodalls-reflections-on-20th-anniversary-of-9-11/
23 https://www.thetimes.com/life-style/property-home/article/jane-goodall-i-try-to-live-as-simple-a-life-as-possible-607pjx7xt?gaa_at=eafs&gaa_n=AWEtsqeGBQ-DGDEHr16dpVzjx2TwiPznmr1LUcIMjnvYh74IOpOHIZcCdkdkGGE71R4=&gaa_ts=69774a93&gaa_sig=8gDxQC2_WFAcwgXx-RMTSQoNHCneOusz0aHOh5huQtJ_LOUe9Vx4u4mBPAidxoKAJqI6nXfppldnCXmI1hQyDg==

24 https://www.washingtonpost.com/climate-solutions/2021/10/19/jane-goodall-book-climate-change/
25 *Jane Goodall: The Woman Who Redefined Man* by Dale Peterson (2006), Mariner Books
26 https://www.youtube.com/watch?v=tv9HG8Tnkio
27 https://news.janegoodall.org/2020/12/30/jane-goodall-hopecast-podcast-ep-1-you-are-reason-for-hope/2/
28 https://imagine5.com/interview/jane-goodall-change-starts-within/?srsltid=AfmBOoq45LcvvcSmYGdsNEWlDHDBUaRkzIDtpm3DhLCQ_K3A6FBICHhx
29 https://time.com/5192249/jane-goodall-sexism-gender-equality-documentary/
30 https://news.lafayette.edu/2013/05/08/transcript-of-jane-goodalls-speech-and-qa-session/
31 https://news.janegoodall.org/2016/04/23/1013/
32 https://news.lafayette.edu/2013/05/08/transcript-of-jane-goodalls-speech-and-qa-session/
33 https://news.janegoodall.org/2016/04/23/1013/
34 https://www.pottsmerc.com/2023/04/12/tv-tinsel-goodall-reflects-on-her-work-which-now-has-inspired-a-fictional-series-for-families/#:~:text=%E2%80%9CAs%20I%20have%20aged%20the,t%20like%20acting%20so%20much.%E2%80%9D
35 https://news.janegoodall.org/2016/04/23/1013/
36 https://www.cherylrosebush.com/blog/when-jane-goodall-endorsed-my-environmental-childrens-book
37 https://www.nytimes.com/2021/10/14/books/review/jane-goodall-by-the-book-interview.html
38 https://www.forbes.com/sites/kionasmith/2025/10/02/8-fascinating-facts-you-might-not-know-about-jane-goodall-and-her-work/

39 https://time.com/5192249/jane-goodall-sexism-gender-equality-documentary/
40 https://digital.sandiego.edu/cgi/viewcontent.cgi?article=1015&context=lecture_series
41 *Reason for Hope: A Spiritual Journey* by Jane Goodall and Phillip Berman (1999), Grand Central Publishing
42 https://www.facebook.com/janegoodall/?locale=en_GB
43 https://www.dumbofeather.com/conversations/jane-goodall-is-a-primatologist/
44 https://time.com/5192249/jane-goodall-sexism-gender-equality-documentary/
45 https://www.wanderlustmagazine.com/inspiration/jane-goodall-interview/
46 https://www.nytimes.com/2015/03/15/magazine/jane-goodall-is-still-wild-at-heart.html#:~:text=Her%20letter%20also%20recorded%2C%20in,and%20hazy%20at%20the%20edge.%E2%80%9D
47 https://news.janegoodall.org/2016/04/23/1013/
48 https://www.wanderlustmagazine.com/inspiration/jane-goodall-interview/
49 https://news.janegoodall.org/2016/08/10/1746/
50 *In the Shadow of Man* by Jane Goodall (1971), W&M
51 https://www.nationalgeographic.com/history/article/jane-goodall-life-career-legacy-chimps

Chapter Two

1 https://www.theguardian.com/science/2023/feb/18/jane-goodall-people-are-surprised-i-have-a-wicked-sense-of-humour
2 https://www.bbc.co.uk/culture/article/20250710-the-woman-who-redefined-chimps-and-human-beings

3 https://www.nationalgeographic.com/history/article/jane-goodall-life-career-legacy-chimps
4 https://www.theguardian.com/science/animal-magic/2014/apr/03/jane-goodall-80-chimp
5 https://www.bbc.co.uk/culture/article/20250710-the-woman-who-redefined-chimps-and-human-beings
6 https://onbeing.org/programs/jane-goodall-what-it-means-to-be-human/
7 https://www.bbc.co.uk/programmes/p029gwnn
8 https://www.livescience.com/animals/land-mammals/from-tool-use-to-warfare-here-are-5-ways-jane-goodall-revolutionized-our-knowledge-of-chimpanzees
9 https://www.ft.com/content/477fc8d7-bcf3-48e9-bc45-cd6e82b6b300
10 https://www.washingtonpost.com/climate-solutions/2021/10/19/jane-goodall-book-climate-change/
11 https://www.independent.co.uk/voices/jane-goodall-tribute-ethologist-chimpanzees-wildlife-conservation-b2837837.html
12 https://www.theguardian.com/science/2023/feb/18/jane-goodall-people-are-surprised-i-have-a-wicked-sense-of-humour
13 https://www.science.org/doi/10.1126/science.282.5397.2184
14 https://awpc.cattcenter.iastate.edu/2025/10/02/un-messenger-of-peace-dr-jane-goodall-addresses-the-climate-assembly-aug-14-2023/
15 https://news.janegoodall.org/2025/04/21/a-message-from-dr-jane-goodall-on-the-passing-of-pope-francis/
16 https://www.ft.com/content/477fc8d7-bcf3-48e9-bc45-cd6e82b6b300
17 https://www.newscientist.com/article/2498651-how-jane-goodall-changed-the-way-we-see-animals-and-the-world/

18 https://www.rotary.org/en/the-conversation-jane-goodall
19 https://www.natgeokids.com/uk/discover/animals/general-animals/jane-goodall-interview/
20 *Jane Goodall: The Woman Who Redefined Man* by Dale Peterson (2006), Mariner Books
21 Ibid
22 https://www.theguardian.com/science/2025/oct/02/dame-jane-goodall-obituary
23 https://www.zsl.org/news-and-events/news/memory-dame-jane-goodall-1934-2025
24 https://www.theguardian.com/science/animal-magic/2014/apr/03/jane-goodall-80-chimp
25 https://www.rotary.org/en/the-conversation-jane-goodall
26 https://www.nationalgeographic.com/history/article/jane-goodall-life-career-legacy-chimps
27 *Africa in My Blood: An Autobiography in Letters: The Early Years* by Jane Goodall (2001), Houghton Mifflin
28 *Jane Goodall: The Woman Who Redefined Man* by Dale Peterson (2006), Mariner Books
29 https://www.theguardian.com/lifeandstyle/2013/feb/23/jane-goodall-interview
30 *Jane Goodall: The Woman Who Redefined Man* by Dale Peterson (2006), Mariner Books
31 https://www.theguardian.com/science/2023/feb/18/jane-goodall-people-are-surprised-i-have-a-wicked-sense-of-humour
32 Ibid
33 https://longneckmanor.com/remembering-jane-goodall-my-30-years-with-an-extraordinary-soul/
34 *Jane Goodall: The Woman Who Redefined Man* by Dale Peterson (2006), Mariner Books

35 https://www.feminist.com/resources/artspeech/interviews/janegoodall.html
36 Ibid
37 *In the Shadow of Man* by Jane Goodall (1971), W&M
38 https://www.latimes.com/archives/la-xpm-2006-oct-01-me-chimps1-story.html
39 *In the Shadow of Man* by Jane Goodall (1971), W&M
40 https://time.com/7322497/jane-goodall-death-hope-legacy/
41 https://whowhatwhy.org/podcast/ahead-of-her-time-my-timeless-conversation-with-jane-goodall-27-years-ago/
42 https://digital.sandiego.edu/cgi/viewcontent.cgi?article=1015&context=lecture_series
43 https://www.rotary.org/en/the-conversation-jane-goodall
44 https://whowhatwhy.org/podcast/ahead-of-her-time-my-timeless-conversation-with-jane-goodall-27-years-ago/

Chapter Three

1 *Jane Goodall: The Woman Who Redefined Man* by Dale Peterson (2006), Mariner Books
2 https://orionmagazine.org/article/the-shadow-of-humanity-and-the-spirit-of-animals/
3 https://onbeing.org/programs/jane-goodall-what-it-means-to-be-human/
4 https://www.latimes.com/archives/la-xpm-2006-oct-01-me-chimps1-story.html
5 https://www.standard.co.uk/news/environment/jane-goodall-planet-earth-london-extinction-regeneration-b1080355.html#:~:text=It%20comes%

20as%20a%20new,often%20treated%20with%20 extreme%20cruelty.&text=%E2%80%9CSecretly% 20filmed%20videos%20reveal%20shocking, fields%20when%20the%20weather%20 permits.%E2%80%9D

6 https://news.janegoodall.org/2023/02/13/happy-valentines-day-from-dr-goodall/

7 https://www.vogue.co.uk/article/prince-harry-jane-goodall-september-2019-issue#:~:text=I%20was%20 going%20to%20Heathrow%20from%20London,I% 20was:%20%E2%80%9COh%2C%20you're%20 just%20like%20my

8 https://www.dumbofeather.com/conversations/jane-goodall-is-a-primatologist/

9 https://observer.co.uk/profile/obituary/article/obituary-jane-goodall

10 https://www.vegetariantimes.com/uncategorized/one-on-one-with-jane-goodall/

11 https://www.amnh.org/learn-teach/curriculum-collections/biodiversity-crisis/profile-jane-goodall

12 https://www.rotary.org/en/the-conversation-jane-goodall

13 https://www.theguardian.com/science/2023/feb/18/jane-goodall-people-are-surprised-i-have-a-wicked-sense-of-humour

14 https://www.natgeokids.com/uk/discover/animals/general-animals/jane-goodall-interview/

15 https://www.rootsnshoots.org.uk/news-from-hq/international-day-of-peace-2025

16 https://guykawasaki.com/jane-goodall-podcast/

17 https://longneckmanor.com/remembering-jane-goodall-my-30-years-with-an-extraordinary-soul/

18 Ibid

19 https://a24films.com/notes/2025/04/ambassador-of-the-heart-with-isaiah-saxon-jane-goodall

20 https://www.dumbofeather.com/conversations/jane-goodall-is-a-primatologist/
21 https://news.janegoodall.org/2025/04/22/dr-jane-goodalls-2025-earth-day-message/
22 https://www.wanderlustmagazine.com/inspiration/jane-goodall-interview/
23 https://www.humaneworld.org/en/all-animals/exclusive-interview-animal-activist-dr-jane-goodall
24 https://news.lafayette.edu/2013/05/08/transcript-of-jane-goodalls-speech-and-qa-session/
25 https://www.feminist.com/resources/artspeech/interviews/janegoodall.html
26 Ibid
27 https://news.janegoodall.org/2016/06/20/1341/#:~:text=Fences%20have%20been%20built%20along,from%20their%20own%20economic%20crisis.
28 https://www.dumbofeather.com/conversations/jane-goodall-is-a-primatologist/
29 *The Book of Hope: A Survival Guide for Trying Times* by Jane Goodall and Douglas Abrams (2021), Viking
30 https://www.washingtonpost.com/climate-solutions/2021/10/19/jane-goodall-book-climate-change/
31 https://www.humaneworld.org/en/all-animals/exclusive-interview-animal-activist-dr-jane-goodall

Chapter Four

1 https://www.ted.com/talks/jane_goodall_what_separates_us_from_chimpanzees
2 https://onbeing.org/programs/jane-goodall-what-it-means-to-be-human/
3 https://digital.sandiego.edu/cgi/viewcontent.cgi?article=1015&context=lecture_series

4 https://archive.ph/Tf3qZ#selection-1821.18-1827.221
5 https://www.humaneworld.org/en/all-animals/exclusive-interview-animal-activist-dr-jane-goodall
6 https://time.com/archive/6665204/out-of-africa/
7 https://www.nytimes.com/2015/03/15/magazine/jane-goodall-is-still-wild-at-heart.html
8 https://www.ted.com/talks/jane_goodall_what_separates_us_from_chimpanzees
9 https://www.latimes.com/archives/la-xpm-2006-nov-19-bk-lewis19-story.html#:~:text=I%20am%20praying%20for%20some,*
10 https://imagine5.com/interview/jane-goodall-change-starts-within/?srsltid=AfmBOoq45LcvvcSmYGdsNEWlDHDBUaRkzIDtpm3DhLCQ_K3A6FBICHhx
11 https://guykawasaki.com/jane-goodall-podcast/
12 https://www.npr.org/transcripts/112795204
13 Ibid
14 https://www.rotary.org/en/the-conversation-jane-goodall
15 https://www.feminist.com/resources/artspeech/interviews/janegoodall.html
16 https://www.thetimes.com/life-style/article/jane-goodall-interview-zqg2c5jc0?gaa_at=eafs&gaa_n=AWEtsqdCVcAkk4c9k2M8j_ADz0oRDCh3Q4ROPmYibQgsTbLHLqpH733w9x6f4FsI2DY=&gaa_ts=69774a93&gaa_sig=wRNmwQc2oRqkGchDni06yGArebKNFaFkqQYr0dUO1b8kAxr5B7sX-Ght-hA6frlis3swz91c_v54VXa__xk_qA==
17 https://www.theguardian.com/science/2010/jan/13/jane-goodall
18 https://news.janegoodall.org/2025/04/22/dr-jane-goodalls-2025-earth-day-message/
19 https://www.globalcitizen.org/en/content/powerful-quotes-from-jane-goodall-australia/

20 https://news.janegoodall.org/2016/06/20/1341/
21 https://news.janegoodall.org/2017/01/20/remembering-my-mentor-robert-hinde/

Chapter Five

1 https://www.washingtonpost.com/climate-solutions/2021/10/19/jane-goodall-book-climate-change/
2 https://www.humaneworld.org/en/all-animals/exclusive-interview-animal-activist-dr-jane-goodall
3 https://www.independent.co.uk/voices/jane-goodall-tribute-ethologist-chimpanzees-wildlife-conservation-b2837837.html
4 https://imagine5.com/interview/jane-goodall-change-starts-within/?srsltid=AfmBOoq45LcvvcSmYGdsNEWlDHDBUaRkzIDtpm3DhLCQ_K3A6FBICHhx
5 https://a24films.com/notes/2025/04/ambassador-of-the-heart-with-isaiah-saxon-jane-goodall
6 https://theconversation.com/jane-goodall-the-gentle-disrupter-whose-research-on-chimpanzees-redefined-what-it-meant-to-be-human-205909
7 https://www.washingtonpost.com/washington-post-live/2021/09/22/transcript-climate-solutions-wildlife-conservation-with-jane-goodall-phd-dbe-paula-kahumbu-phd/
8 https://www.washingtonpost.com/climate-solutions/2021/10/19/jane-goodall-book-climate-change/
9 https://amatranscripts.com/ama/jane_goodall_2017-09-13.html
10 https://www.wanderlustmagazine.com/inspiration/jane-goodall-interview/
11 Ibid
12 https://archive.ph/Tf3qZ#selection-1903.21-1909.110

13 https://www.theguardian.com/science/2023/feb/18/jane-goodall-people-are-surprised-i-have-a-wicked-sense-of-humour
14 https://archive.ph/Tf3qZ#selection-1833.0-1835.136
15 https://www.thetimes.com/life-style/article/jane-goodall-interview-zqg2c5jc0?gaa_at=eafs&gaa_n=AWEtsqdCVcAkk4c9k2M8j_ADz0oRDCh3Q4ROPmYibQgsTbLHLqpH733w9x6f4FsI2DY=&gaa_ts=69774a93&gaa_sig=wRNmwQc2oRqkGchDni06yGArebKNFaFkqQYr0dUO1b8kAxr5B7sX-Ght-hA6frlis3swz91c_v54VXa__xk_qA==
16 https://www.belfasttelegraph.co.uk/life/weekend/when-i-heard-they-planned-another-film-i-thought-come-on-i-just-dont-have-the-time/36351338.html
17 https://granta.com/the-covid-19-pandemic/
18 https://www.independent.co.uk/climate-change/news/jane-goodall-interview-animal-markets-wildlife-trafficking-a9458611.html
19 https://news.janegoodall.org/2022/01/04/dr-goodall-remembers-desmond-tutu/
20 https://news.janegoodall.org/2025/09/22/world-rhino-day-2025/
21 https://www.nytimes.com/2025/10/01/climate/jane-goodall-interviews.html
22 https://rootsandshoots.global/dr-jane-goodalls-message-for-international-day-of-peace-2024/
23 https://www.bbc.co.uk/news/articles/c93qvqx5y01o
24 https://www.npr.org/transcripts/112795204

Chapter Six

1 https://www.theguardian.com/science/2021/oct/20/jane-goodall-on-fires-floods-frugality-and-the-good-fight-people-have-to-change-from-within

2 https://www.butlernature.com/2025/11/13/jane-goodalls-memorial/

3 https://time.com/7333425/jane-goodall-funeral-leonardo-dicaprio/

4 https://www.washingtonpost.com/washington-post-live/2021/09/22/transcript-climate-solutions-wildlife-conservation-with-jane-goodall-phd-dbe-paula-kahumbu-phd/

5 https://imagine5.com/interview/jane-goodall-change-starts-within/?srsltid=AfmBOoq45LcvvcSmYGdsNEWlDHDBUaRkzIDtpm3DhLCQ_K3A6FBICHhx

6 https://www.npr.org/transcripts/112795204

7 https://digital.sandiego.edu/cgi/viewcontent.cgi?article=1015&context=lecture_series

8 https://www.natgeokids.com/uk/discover/animals/general-animals/jane-goodall-interview/

9 https://www.washingtonpost.com/climate-solutions/2021/10/19/jane-goodall-book-climate-change/

10 https://www.independent.co.uk/voices/jane-goodall-tribute-ethologist-chimpanzees-wildlife-conservation-b2837837.html